One Less

GU00729053

What is life like without alcohol? Is it even worth considering? And could YOU cope?

An awareness, awakening and thought provoking book aimed at people contemplating curtailing or even giving up their drinking forever

– and a book that might just change your life!

Julian Kirkman-Page

After 40 years of drinking and ending up a total mess with type 2 diabetes, high blood pressure, gout and truthfully expecting to be dead not long after the age of 56, one day in 2012 I decided to quit alcohol forever. Without resorting to drugs, rehab or any outside help I've never touched a drop since, and have never been so wonderfully healthy, happy or contented in my life.

But before that fateful day, **I never wanted to give up drinking**, I loved drinking, and I couldn't envisage life without the daily joy of bottles of wine, cider and the occasional gin. So what is it really like when you throw the alcohol crutch away, and how have I coped with what I expected to be a life full of daily challenges, stress, regret, boredom and witnessing the laughter and the fun times steadily fade into distant memory? What would it be like for you?

This book is a wake-up call for anyone like me who thought there was no life after alcohol!

I hope to show you through my own experience and confirmed through that of others kind enough to share their experiences with me, what life is actually like without drink; help you think for yourself what your own life will be like without drink; wake you to all the things you are currently missing out on without realising it because drink is getting in the way; and help you understand what your life might be like and what you will miss if you simply carry on as you are today.

My story

Questions for you

Hilarious drinking tales and escapades

Thoughts and challenges

Daily aspects discussed

The first day of a new life

Suggested ways forward

Dedicated to my darling wife Lolly,

for putting up with someone I wouldn't have given the time of day

Mallard Publishing

Contents

Introduction

I never wanted to give up drinking,

in fact I couldn't imagine life without drink apart from it being boring and without purpose, after all, why work hard and give it your all if you can't then enjoy your favourite tipple when you feel like it. But in 2012 I **did** give up drinking - forever. Despite my previous misgivings I now wish I'd given up drinking years before and perhaps never even started at all. I don't wish this for any medical reasons (I've been very lucky and the damage I did to myself has seemingly repaired or resolved itself), but purely because I now realise that having wasted all those years drinking, I have already missed out on so much that might have happened in my life, and that I could have been doing but wasn't, so I didn't, because I was so beholden to this damn chemical we call alcohol. Now I'm free of its grip I'm so positive about everything in my life going forward, I wouldn't be tempted to have even the tiniest sip no matter what fortune sent my way, good or bad.

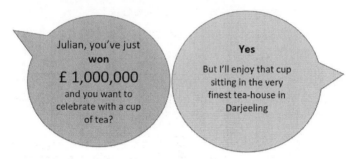

So this isn't a 'how to' guide, it's a 'why to' guide, and hopefully an enjoyable and amusing one too.

So what have I achieved so far since I quit alcohol?

You will find in this book that I don't preach on about all the harm alcohol does to you, after all you don't need to look far to find a wealth of all that negative information you probably don't want to hear anyway. But as part of this introduction it's worth me briefly summarising what I have tangibly achieved since I stopped being an alcoholic, not by way of showing off but just to emphasise what a phenomenal difference quitting alcohol can make and has made:-

- I have resolved the type 2 diabetes I had been diagnosed with, something my GP said couldn't happen. So yes, type 2 diabetes can be beaten and if you have this terrible condition this fact alone might be sufficient for you to want to change your lifestyle.
- I have got rid of my high blood pressure and no longer have to take tablets.
- I have also got rid of my high cholesterol and no longer have to take tablets.
- My heart rate is athlete status and that means a healthy strong heart that should hopefully last me for decades.
- I have completely got rid of the crippling gout I have suffered with for countless years and although I was reluctant to admit it, was a direct result of my drinking.
- Without trying I have lost two stone (28 pounds) in weight, and I am now firmly in the healthy BMI range for a male of my height and build. It just goes to show how much hidden sugar there is in alcohol.
- My skin has improved markedly and I have got rid of the psoriasis I have suffered with from childhood.
- I have never felt so healthy or been so fit and active since I was a young man.
- I feel at least ten years younger and I am told I look so much younger as well, which of

course makes me feel fantastic.

- I have a wonderful, happy and harmonious relationship with my loved ones and I know I am a much nicer, calmer, thoughtful and caring person to be around.
- I have never achieved so much in such a short space of time and every day is productive in every way.
- I have saved shedloads of money.
- My life is stress free, I am happy, I am content and I have a new positive philosophy on life.
- I have far more quality time for myself and for others.
- I have discovered a sense of freedom I thought I had lost with my childhood.
- My self-esteem has risen massively and I am incredibly proud of having quit drinking.

But most importantly of all, I no longer see living until retirement age as being an achievement in itself, and instead I realistically expect to live well into my nineties. That is an extra thirty plus, healthy, happy, wiser years I have bought myself. In other words, giving up drinking has turned my life around completely!

But looking back I also never thought I would admit to being an alcoholic.

You will learn why I classed myself as an alcoholic later in the book, but the very word 'alcoholic' is often portrayed as a dirty word and labels you for life as being a failure and a loser doesn't it? Well no it shouldn't and no it doesn't! I'm one of an increasing number of voices who are sensible enough to break with tradition and say you are NOT an alcoholic for life just because you faced up to facts and admitted to being one. That despite what some organisations portray, quitting drinking does NOT mean every day of your life will be a challenge of your will versus alcohol, and that you do NOT need to spend the rest of your life as part of some on-going support programme, unless of course you want that kind of thing. I can confidently say these things because I have 'been there and done that'. I have been an alcoholic and now I'm not, and I have an ever increasing number of readers of my 'how to quit alcohol' book who have also been alcoholics and now they're not.

It's an important point to get across right at the start because the term alcoholic puts many people off reading books like this or seeking help. Many people I meet are reluctant or even scared to give themselves a label which has become so stigmatised and often by the very organisations that are supposedly trying to help. If you don't like the term alcoholic then don't use it and just admit to yourself to having a drink issue instead. If by the time you have finished this book you want to quit drinking forever like I did, then the end result is the same anyway and whether or not you were/are an alcoholic is irrelevant. So don't let the term hold you back and wherever I use it in this book simply replace it with something you feel more comfortable with.

Who is this book aimed at?

Since publishing my book on how to quit alcohol, I talk to and receive a lot of correspondence from people whose lives are negatively impacted one way or another by alcohol. Perhaps because I have 'come out' and gone public as having been an alcoholic, they feel able to share with me this massive issue affecting them but previously kept hidden away, and still a considered a taboo subject by so many and so much of society. Many of the people I hear from don't themselves have a drink problem but instead live with, are close to, or have in their family someone who is or probably is an alcoholic, and who they desperately want to help. Unfortunately for whatever reason that person either won't listen, or they simply won't accept that they have an issue with drink, or they know they have a problem but see it as **their** problem so want to be left alone. They probably don't even realise how their own drinking affects the lives of others to such an extent. That 'person' might be you.

Some people I talk to just want to know what it is like living sober. It really is a stretch of the imagination to picture getting through each day with the sure knowledge you won't **ever** be drinking again. If you read that sentence again, what will most likely immediately spring to mind are things like birthdays, weddings, funerals, Christmas, beach holidays, and the countless other annual events where drinking and getting smashed is an integral part.

Question:

As you are today, can you truly imagine a forever sober life?

If I had been asked that same question three years ago, I would only have been able to conceive such a thing if I had been a castaway on a desert island, and even then I would have been hoping to find a barrel of something alcoholic washed up, or looked to how I could distil or brew something from coconut palms. If you fall into this camp, hopefully you will find the book enlightening.

Once someone finally recognises for themselves that they have a drink problem **and** they determine to change their life and quit alcohol, they can either help themselves or my book 'I Don't Drink!' and many other resources besides can really assist. But that someone needs to get firmly to that wanting to give up stage before **anyone** can help. I know from my own experience that I had to **want** to change my life before I considered quitting alcohol, and that until I decided that fact, no amount of health warnings or coercion from anybody would have done (or did do) the slightest bit of good.

Yes I knew I was drinking a lot, but then everything I read in the press or heard about alcohol seemed to state that fifty per cent of people in my age bracket, or with a stressful job, or even just males in general had a similar drink problem, so I wasn't unique and therefore didn't need to do anything about it. I also read somewhere that women were more likely to be secret alcoholics than men. To my mind it is these very types of statistic, supposedly aimed at making people reduce their alcohol intake that compound the issue and just provide yet more excuses not to confront the problem. It's a bit like the global obesity problem, there is such a huge comfort factor to be had from knowing that half the Western world is fat, why make the effort to be slim if 'no-one' else can be bothered.

What's the point of giving up drinking, after all it seems half the World has a drink problem. I'm not unique.

This book is therefore aimed primarily at the person who **needs** to quit or at least drastically limit their drinking, but who is either ignoring the fact, sweeping the issue under the carpet as my wife would say, or who can't make that final leap and decide to actually quit. That need might be driven by health, work, or relationship issues, or simply the inkling of an idea that life might actually be better and more fulfilling if they drank less. If that person is you, you probably can't imagine what life would be like without alcohol other than for it to be deathly boring, unless you like wearing uniform and playing a brass instrument. You may even have the extreme view of 'what is the point of living if you can't enjoy a good drink', or you're simply swanning through life content with the mess you are becoming but oblivious to the opportunities passing you by, and to the pain and hurt your drinking may be causing others around you. If this all sounds a bit blunt and in your face, well it probably needs to be, but don't throw away or delete the book just yet.

On a softer note, if you have actually bought this book for yourself then at least you recognise you have an issue. You have likely been told by others either recently or in the past to do something about your drinking, perhaps even accompanied by an 'or else' statement, or you may have been advised by your GP to cut down or cut out alcohol altogether. You might even have scared yourself into realising something might have to change by perhaps being so drunk you lost a huge chunk of your day and you don't know where it went. But whatever your reason for reading thus far, I bet I know one thing about you:

> You **don't really want** to give up drink!
> Because I know I didn't.

If instead of you buying it, someone has given this book to you it comes with a message. It is certainly because they care about you and they want a better life for you, but also, if they are close to you, they want a better life for themselves as well. So please don't dismiss the message they are sending you – at least read the book first!

How to use this book

So what is life like without booze? – A drinker's tale.

Following a brief background as to why I wrote this book, the first section talks about my own relationship with drink and is aimed at creating some sort of affinity with your own situation as it relates to alcohol. I discuss how much I drank, how wedded I was to alcohol, what made me finally decide to quit, and what convinced me I had been an alcoholic even though this realisation only came **after** I had given up drink. I also talk about mine and other people's attitudes to non-drinkers which can often be a person's main reason not to quit.

Section two - a voyage of self-discovery

The second section looks at some specific aspects of everyday life to see how we can map them to what your day looks like. I include subjects such as work, money, health including weight loss, fitness, entertainment, hobbies and past-times, travel and holidays, food and drink, friends and family, and a small chapter on philosophy. There are a lot of searching questions in this section geared towards making you think about your life as it currently is, and more importantly how it could be if you decide to quit alcohol.

The following chapter of the book asks you to place yourself in someone else's shoes and questions how well you think you could live with yourself as you are now.

Finally, I describe what it was like on the very first day I gave up drinking forever, and if by the time you have read that far you decide to positively do something about reducing or hopefully taking the easier path and stopping your own alcohol intake forever, I offer suggestions as to how to proceed.

Altogether there are over 50 questions in the book for you to ask yourself, five challenges to undertake and a couple of tasks to consider.

As you work your way through the book, especially in section two, you might want to **highlight or list** benefits and issues from quitting drinking that relate to you and your life. You might instead want to do this after you have read the book and go through it again, but either way, do try and focus on them as they arise.

Let's start with that brief background as to why I wrote this book...

Background to the book

In the chapters that follow you will notice that I deliberately don't harp on about the medical reasons for quitting alcohol because you are not stupid, and as a heavy drinker you already know what damage alcohol can cause you, and you will already be feeling the effects - there is also ample evidence of the dangers of alcohol cited in the press nearly every day (together with adverts of beautifully healthy looking people having a wonderful time drinking on a yacht or at a smart party). But if you are like I was, you probably don't care enough about yourself to want to take the negative message to heart, or at least you don't care enough **yet,** and you probably don't see yourself as others do. When you are pissed you might even see yourself as one of those beautifully healthy people.

To be really blunt, you may be so beholden to alcohol you actually think you're past the point of caring, in which case the hooded spectre awaits you like it did my brother Paul who drank himself to death in 2008 at the age of fifty-six.

My brother Paul

It was thinking of Paul that to an extent inspired this book, that's him on the right of the picture with me. I know everyone says you shouldn't look back on events, but when Paul was at his worst, had I known what I know now and been the person I now am, I could perhaps have saved his life.

Not having seen him for some time and then discovering him to be in a dreadful condition through alcoholism, I had somehow managed to get him to agree to go into rehab just to get him off the streets. I didn't know anything about rehab myself but I had heard of it through a work colleague who went to rehab to cure his own alcohol problem. What Paul really needed was someone with him who understood what living without alcohol was going to be like - someone who had been there and done that and who could picture for him the wonderland that awaited him just a short space of time away, if only he would let alcohol lose its grip on him. Instead all that was being offered at the rehab he went to were endless 'heard it all before' health tutorials, a locked space so he couldn't escape to the pub with his alcoholic mates, and an alien environment that bore no relation to the life he would have to cope with once he was finally allowed to go home. Even the reformed alcoholics he was being introduced to were shaky in the extreme, topped up with drugs and other alcohol substitutes, and only one step away from returning to their old ways. Hardly inspiring.

I now think the whole future he was being offered was too bleak for him.

> 'Once an alcoholic always an alcoholic', my brother was told and, 'for the rest of your life every day will be a challenge, but with our continued help you will be able to face life and keep the bottle at bay.'
>
> **What a load of bollocks I now know this is.**

'Once an alcoholic always an alcoholic' he was told, 'and for the rest of your life every day will be a challenge. But with our continued help you will be able to face life and beat the bottle.'

This has to be such a negative message – it almost says you might as well keep on drinking and accept you are going to have a much shorter life.

At one stage I even thought of taking Paul in to live with me and somehow locking him away from booze myself, but although I hadn't yet adopted the label I was an alcoholic too, so how could I expect to keep drink from him and moralise to him if I was going to be sneaking out into the garden for a glass of wine every half hour. In any event I had no idea what he would be going through or what he would be thinking. For all I knew alcohol really was addictive and he would be like what I imagined some heroin addict to be in withdrawal, even to the extent he might need restraining to stop him hurting himself. I had only ever given up smoking and that was hard enough, and remember, I certainly didn't want to give up drink, so a solution that involved me also quitting alcohol was just too impossible to contemplate.

> It's not a case of what you think you know about quitting alcohol, but what you haven't thought of yet, because you haven't been there, and you haven't done that yet!

Now I know different. Now I know how fantastic and fulfilling and free life is without drink. Now I know that despite all that the experts may say, alcohol is not addictive, it is a habit that can be easily broken, and it is the thought processes associated with drinking that are the addictive part and you can easily beat them - we are all strong enough to do that when we put our mind to it. Now I know I could have taken Paul under my wing, worked through the methodology I used on myself with him, and saved him.

But I also know before I could have done that he would have had to **want** to be saved. And that is what the nub of this book is really about - showing you through my own experience and confirmed through that of others kind enough to share their experiences with me, what life is actually like without drink; making you think for yourself what your own life will be like without drink; wakening you to all the things you are currently missing out on without realising it because drink is getting in the way; and making you understand what your life might be like if you simply carry on as you are.

If you take the time to consider and even answer the questions I ask in this book, there are some great things to discover about yourself and some not so nice things to contemplate too. There are stories and things that will hopefully make you laugh, but there may be things that will upset you and might make you sad, especially when you look back on things **you have already missed out on**, but that can't be helped, although it can be stopped from happening again.

Finally, when you've finished reading this book you may simply decide to ignore your own thoughts and imaginings and carry on as you are. Or you may decide to listen to your inner self, look back on what you have learnt and decide that just like I did, you want to quit alcohol forever and do something massively positive for yourself. You will hopefully also believe me when I say that those difficult to conceive without alcohol events that I brought to mind earlier like birthdays, weddings, funerals, Christmas, and beach holidays won't be difficult or impossible to face sober, because if you do take my approach and quit alcohol forever, you really won't miss it at all!

I hope I can provide that positive spark, because unless you take that latter option, believe me, you really won't know what you <u>are</u> missing. But let's think only positive and by the time you finish reading this book you WILL want to quit alcohol, you WILL be convinced you won't miss drinking once you knock it on the head, and you WILL know for sure that life will be so much better without booze. If we can get to that stage, then the first and biggest barrier to quitting alcohol will already be behind you. Let's begin…

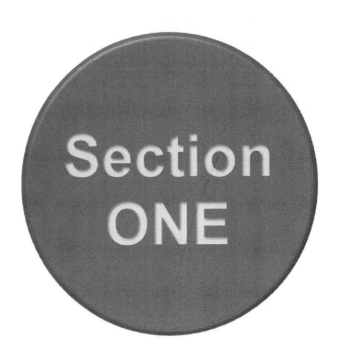

Section
ONE

So what is life like without booze?

A drinker's tale.

It is too glib just to say it's fantastic although from my own perspective it would be an honest statement. I also have to admit that I enjoyed drinking and had some fantastic times too, and some of the funniest things that have ever happened to me were when I was drunk. I deliberately include some of those stories in this book to prove I am a real person and to let you know that I really have 'been there and done that'. What I have found incredible is that I don't miss any of that, not for a second, and although I do have regrets, especially for the things I know I could have done had I led a sober or at least a more sober life, I can't change any of that, so the regrets are only fleeting. I would rather spend the rest of my life looking forward and making sure I make the most of every second that comes along. Many who know me and work with me label me as being incredibly laid back, and I suppose I am, perhaps the new life you feel when you quit alcohol is like being told you no longer have cancer or a similar life threatening disease, hopefully I will never know.

I have partitioned my own story into sub-sections

based on different aspects of my life, both work and personal, and I discuss in each what has changed since I quit alcohol, what if anything I missed through being a drinker and what if anything I miss now I no longer am. The idea is to get you thinking about your own life from various perspectives and how it might differ and have differed if alcohol wasn't involved. I will start with something I used to really enjoy, but at the same time didn't – bear with me, it's a long chapter, but you will hopefully see what I am getting at and maybe you can relate to the same feelings. It will also serve to tell you a little more about me.

A quiet night alone

My wife and I have been together for over twenty-five years but because before I met her I had already had two failed marriages she only finally agreed to marry me six years ago. For a time we were lucky enough to have two homes, one a flat by the sea and the other a small cottage in the country, literally in the middle of nowhere. I have always loved open spaces and I eventually found the flat very restricting, especially as it only had one living room and no garden. I also used to love barbecue food and not having anywhere to cook outdoors was frustrating. For that reason whilst my wife remained at the flat, I took to living at the cottage during the week, which also happened to mean a nicer train journey up to London where I worked in the insurance industry.

As a drinker, living alone meant I could get drunk with my City colleagues after work (as well as most lunchtimes) and get home still smashed without having to worry about upsetting anyone, or getting nagged. The one big pain was getting from the train station to the cottage in the evening without drink driving. Having lost my licence for just such a reason many years previously I was loathe to repeat the experience. Instead I would either walk or cycle the three miles home which was mostly uphill.

Sometimes this would be quite a pleasant journey, especially in the summer. But if it was cold or raining it would be miserable and on more than one occasion, being at the end of my tether, I threw the heavy bag I was carrying with my computer laptop in it into a field to be picked up the next day if I could remember where. Sometimes it was raining so hard, and my coat and suit would get so drenched I would arrive at my front door looking like a drowned rat. If you wonder why I never caught a taxi, there weren't any, the nearest large town being fifteen miles away, and in any event I couldn't afford the extortionate fare they would have charged to come out and get me. The cottage was also so remote, in the three years I lived there alone I was only ever once passed by a car I could thumb a lift from. But it was worth the struggle home because once inside, and assuming I had left any in the fridge from the night before or had remembered to buy some before I left the City, I could reward myself with yet more wine to drink.

I have said I am an outdoors person and assuming it wasn't too late, I would ignite some charcoal to get the barbecue going (I had built a lean-to area especially for this purpose), and look forward to a dinner of sausages and baked beans washed down with cider and white wine.

Whilst the charcoal did its thing I would spend my time in the garden relaxing with my drink, even if that meant wearing a coat, scarf and hat. The garden itself was a wonderful place to unwind in. On one side was another cottage where an old lady lived and who rarely emerged from her mouse-like existence (apart to feed bread to the local rats she had made pets of), on two other sides were dark forests where huge deer roamed (and imaginary wild boar waited to kill you if you had had sufficient to drink), and on the fourth side a meadow which sloped down to a woodland and a small brook. Being so isolated I would walk round our tree filled garden, watch the stars come out and welcome the night's dark embrace. Often I had work to do, especially during the period I was studying for a degree with the Open University, but I would put this off until later in the evening, promising myself I would focus better once I had eaten.

If I was walking around the garden I would always carry a glass of wine with me and slug the wine back every time I stopped. Naturally I kept running out of wine and would have to return to my point of departure for a top-up. Not being overlooked, I knew I was never being watched and so could have perhaps carried the bottle around with me instead, but this felt so much like being an alcoholic I was reluctant to do this. I would lie to myself that I wasn't a drunkard and that I didn't have a drink problem, and even convince myself I could give up booze at the drop of a hat if I wanted. On occasion I would get so drunk waiting for my sausages to cook I would trip and spill some wine or even feel woozy and know I was very very drunk, but the only concern was that I would run out of drink, there never being a sufficient back up supply available – it would just have been drunk anyway.

At one stage I joined one of those wine clubs because of the offer of a free case of wine if you ordered two mixed cases (of crap they couldn't otherwise sell). I thought it would be nice to have a wine-rack full of bottles to admire and drool over and that it would provide a ready-made stock of wine for weeks to come. All I did was drink twice as much as usual, quickly run out of wine and have an empty wine rack to stare at, and annoy my wife who was fed up with me throwing money away for no good reason.

After the meal, I would promise myself to do any work I had after yet another glass of wine and I would listen to music, either on the hi-fi inside, or on a portable CD player in the garden. If the weather conditions were suitable, we had a fire pit on the edge of the forest at the end of the garden and I would go and sit there with a small fire of logs blazing and contemplate. If I was doing that I **would** take a bottle with me.

It was now I would fill my head with dreams. Dreams of who I wanted to be, who I wished I had been, of things I wished I had done, and things I wished to do. Most often the music would set the mood and no work would get done that night:

The sounds of the 70's:

Elton John's music would take me back to my late teens, especially his early albums such as *Madman across the Water, Goodbye Yellow Brick Road*, and *Don't Shoot Me I'm only the Piano Player*.

My teenage years were a time when I should have felt I could do and be anything I wanted. Unfortunately I never knew what I wanted to be or do! I had no specific ambition at school so nothing in particular to aim for, and was eventually thrown out with just three O'levels; I had even started an A'level course but only Art and History of Art because these were deemed easy, and it didn't matter if you couldn't be bothered to turn up. I ended up working in a shop just to avoid being thrown out of home as well. My dad was a chartered accountant and spent most of his working life saying how much he hated his job, so he hardly inspired me to follow in his footsteps. My elder brother Paul had achieved fewer qualifications than I had and was also thrown out of school. His one ambition was to be a racing driver and he even gave it a brief go until he ran out of the small legacy he had been left by a distant great aunt – I had spent my share by the time I was eighteen on clubbing, women and booze.

But listening to the music I remembered how I enjoyed youthful dreams of success, even if I was doing nothing towards fulfilling them. I remember wishing I was a black belt at karate so I never had to worry about being beaten up by skinheads again, but I did nothing about learning. I could never be bothered to go through the years of training to be a black belt, I wanted the skills and the belt to be with me in one magic flash. I was like that with a lot of things. I remember wishing I was already a successful businessman with a huge office and a secretary and a big fancy car parked outside, probably a Jag, but I did nothing about that other than dream. I didn't want to have to 'waste' my time working my way up any ladder. I remember wishing I was a famous soldier of senior rank and with all the girls hero-worshipping me, but I never bothered to find out about joining up and had hated being a bottom rank able seaman in the Naval Corps at school. And I even remember wishing I was studying for some hugely academic degree at university rather than working in a shop, but I had missed my chance, and I would have had to go back to school, start again, and work hard for at least three more years to even get the opportunity back, and I wasn't about to do that.

As the drink soothed me and took my cares away and the music worked its magic I could believe I had actually done the things in my life that I hadn't. I **was** a karate black belt, I **was** a retired Colonel in the SAS with fantastic stories to tell, I **was** a rich businessman, and I **did** have a degree after all. It didn't matter that I would never really be or have these things because I was drunk, and I could worry about reality the next day when I was sober, and I would be too busy coping with everyday life to care. In fact I had a massive number of things to celebrate about my life but I wasn't thinking clearly. Perhaps a psychoanalyst might suggest the hidden guilt of having wasted so much opportunity **and continuing to waste that opportunity** was getting in the way.

A 1975 song – Make me smile (come up and see me) Steve Harley and Cockney Rebel.

Whilst mentioning music and the 70's, I had to mention this song. More than any other song I have ever heard it reminds me instantly of mega-drinking, I can even vividly picture the circumstances when I first heard it.

I was eighteen years old and on holiday with a mate of mine in Majorca. We were staying at a very large budget-priced hotel, one of the ones with over five hundred rooms and packed with mostly English holiday makers. I remember they had a hut in the hotel grounds near the swimming pool that housed a juke box and some pinball machines, but that they used to close the hut after ten p.m. so as not to keep little kids awake. One evening my mate and I were so drunk we broke open the door after midnight, turned everything on and played pinball listening to this great song on full volume over and over again. We had brought some beers with us and after a while two very violent looking Scots boys joined us to add to the noise and to have a pinball competition. Needless to say we got so paralytic we broke some of the machines and a load of young tough looking Spanish waiters came to 'sort us out'. One big punch-up later (my friend and I just stood idly by and watched the Scots guys do the fighting) the Spanish were either floating in the hotel swimming pool or unconscious, my friend had fallen through a glass door whilst laughing too much and had cut his hand so badly it needed fifteen stitches the next day (that evening he simply wrapped it in a towel and from the mess in the bedroom, he probably lost two pints of blood overnight), and I had reached 'full' to the extent my head was spinning and I joined the Spanish in an unconscious heap. The last thing I remember of that evening as I passed out was that song still playing in the background.

Whenever I hear it now I can instantly feel the balmy Mediterranean warmth of that evening, hear the background tinkle of breaking glass, and taste the memorable flavour of warm San Miguel beer. What a great evening that was.

Question:

Which one song most brings to mind a drunken event for you?

ELO:

Songs by The Electric Light Orchestra would give me a buzz, especially from the *Out of the Blue* album. I would pace around the garden listening to this music or even dance and play air guitar to some of the rock tracks, spilling wine or cider liberally. ELO took me back to my early twenties, a time when I had already been married and divorced for the first time and was living and working in South Africa. That had been a time of massive opportunity for me, most of which I drank away, too stupid to stay sober enough to see what the World was offering. Although I am lucky enough to be incredibly happy with my life now, I often get asked what I would tell my twenty year old self if I could go back in time, and it truly is 'drink less', or if you can't regulate your drinking (which I never could) 'don't drink at all.' I would say to myself 'drink later on in your life if you really feel you have to' (trying to convince the twenty year old me to never drink would have been an impossibility) 'but stay sober enough to capture the opportunities that come your way when you are in your prime.' I wouldn't be able to listen to too much ELO before I would start to berate myself. I would decide to do big positive things from now on and want to start straight away, but of course being drunk that was impossible, so instead I would have to slow the pace down and put on something like Van Morrison or some Pink Floyd instead.

Van Morrison:

I came across the music of Van the Man travelling through Africa in a Land Rover with a Rhodesian pal of mine. That was a year spent in deepest darkest Africa living by my wits and with zero responsibility not even really for myself. Africa back in the late 1970's - early 80's was a continent where you really could be anything you wanted if you made the effort, I am sure it still is. When I lived in South Africa I had progressed from working in a shop in the UK to running a department store in Johannesburg with five hundred staff, purely by virtue of being white, polite and well spoken. I then became an insurance broker because the opportunity arose. On my travels I ran a tobacco farm in Malawi for a while, I nearly became the owner of a major hotel and a night club, and I was nearly shot whilst doing a short spell as a spy in Mozambique.

It was sitting by a night-time camp fire in the middle of a Zambian forest that I first fell in love with the music of Van Morrison, listening to Astral Weeks, smoking a large joint and sipping tea. We had speakers and a sound system rigged into the Land Rover and wherever we parked we would put on some music which also helped to scare the wild animals away. It also attracted local tribesmen keen to enjoy the music and become our servants for the duration, in return for clothes we were content to part with, medicines, and luxuries such as soap. We had very few possessions with us, very little money, and no set itinerary either in our journey or in our lives. It was that classic period in one's life when if a chance arises you take it. I'm sure if someone had offered me the chance to join a one-way mission to Mars I would have grabbed the opportunity without a moment's hesitation.

Listening to that same music at the cottage brought those happy memories flooding back and made me sad that all life can't be as contented and trouble free. I had since caught glimpses of it when I'd been on safari in Kenya with my current wife, especially round a fire or by a river in the evening, just listening to the call of the wild, smelling the raw beauty of Mankind's birthplace, and wondering at the majesty of the Milky Way above. Sitting in an armchair getting drunk and being alone I would sometimes dull my senses to the point that If I had never woken up I don't think I'd have noticed the transition. Pink Floyd would sometimes bring me to tears, not of sadness but of the beauty of everything passing me by and for lost times. My life was very much a mixture of contentment and acceptance tinged with regret.

Classical:

I am not in any way a classics buff, but I do adore the intense feelings that classical music can invoke.

Organ music would make me wish I was a closet

musician sitting in a cathedral and surprising all who know me by suddenly giving an amazing rendition of Bach's Toccata and Fugue in D minor on the grand organ. It's still an objective I hold dear.

Not quite a classic but Ennio Morricone's music score from the film *Once upon a time in the West* is incredibly haunting. It always made me want to have achieved great things. Tchaikovsky is another composer whose music I could listen to all day, invoking mood swings from happiness to awe as I pictured the incredible times his 1812 overture represented, when so many people were slaughtered on the whim of the Emperor Napoleon, a man who had set out to achieve magnificence, and for a considerable period of his life, attained just that.

I never got depressed listening to the music and drinking, or not that I recognised any such symptoms in myself. I would get very lonely however, and many times I wished I hadn't had a drink so I could drive over and be with my wife. I didn't telephone her late in the evening either, and for a similar reason, I didn't want to sound paralytic on the phone which would have meant revealing to myself something was very wrong, and that I had a problem to face. Even straying too far from the cottage on my bicycle or going for a walk would lead me too far away from the bottle that without me realising, had become my crutch, and there were no pubs nearby. I would instead think of the things I might one day achieve, know secretly that I would never achieve any of them, and go to bed both happy and sad, but with an ever hopeful philosophy of 'who knows what tomorrow might bring' and the secret knowledge that I wouldn't remember much of the evening anyway.

Waking up

I was really scared of giving up drink

What would I feel in the evening without the comfort of alcohol? What would I do with myself, I couldn't just keep going for endless walks? How would I sleep if I hadn't numbed my brain before going to bed? Would I be fretting and shaking like I had been when I gave up smoking? Would I pace the room like a caged lion and go mad? After a lifetime of having an alcohol comfort blanket it was all too alien to contemplate.

To give you an idea of how much I was drinking in the evening, my wife and I used my empty wine bottles turned upside down, to create a border along the path in our garden. In just two years I created over 80 metres of path edging. At 7.5 cm width per bottle, that exceeds 1,000 bottles of wine. On top of that I was also drinking cider, just so the wine lasted longer and went further. Remember, all this was in addition to what I was drinking at lunchtime and after work.

Question:

Let's get it out of the way early on because I am

---

completely honest with YOU in this book, about everything. How much do you drink?

I am not bothered about how many units are 'ok' for you to drink because if you ever quit completely like I have, then the number of units becomes immaterial. What you need to be frank with yourself about is how much you really truly hand-on-heart drink. Not what you would tell a doctor, or tell someone who started to look shocked when you began to reveal the extent of your drinking, but the truth for yourself. That will help you read the rest of this book because when I ask you other questions you won't be hiding behind excuses or any fake self-belief that you don't drink too much. Why not write down how much you drink and add it up. You can copy my example in the following table. I have left room for your own entries:-

Table 1: average weekly volume of alcohol consumed (conservative estimate)

		Me			You	
Day	Wine (glasses)	Beer/Cider (pints)	Spirits (measures)	Wine (glasses)	Beer/Cider (pints)	Spirits (measures)
Monday	8	3.5				
Tuesday	8	3.5				
Wednesday	8	3.5				
Thursday	8	3.5				
Friday	10	4.0				
Saturday	8	5.0	1			
Sunday	8	3.5				
Totals	58	26.5	1			

Note: 5 glasses of wine = 1 bottle.

*Incidentally if my total doesn't look too bad compared to yours (it might of course on the other hand be massively bigger than yours) I realised in putting this table together it relates very much to the final three years of my drinking. If you were to look at the previous ten years you could add **at least** one bottle of wine per day to the total and 5 more spirit measures on a Saturday night!*

Almost always, late in the evening I would promise myself that the next day I was going to change things in my life and start by not drinking. I remember promising to turn my dreams and fantasies into reality. I would work harder and not waste half the day in a wine bar; I would take up a hobby or activity that added something to my life; I would get fit; I would give more of my time and myself to my family instead of hiding away at the cottage; I would stop drinking, I would stop drinking, I would stop drinking.

The next morning assuming I wasn't hungover (which I rarely was – I had a great capacity for alcohol and only drank reasonably priced booze, never cheap muck) my resolve to give up alcohol completely would change to cutting down my drinking, and I would already be planning my day around my first drink.

'I will just have two glasses of wine at lunchtime' I

would say to myself, 'so I will be OK to drive to the station today. Then, as I still have half a bottle of wine left in the fridge, that will do for tonight. If I stick to that I will only have consumed one bottle of wine all day and I can be really quite proud of myself.'

By lunchtime however, the resolve had generally gone and I would end up smashed, have to leave the car at the station and walk home. Thinking of that half bottle at home in the fridge I would also make sure before I left the City I bought at least one if not two more bottles of wine just in case.

To be honest I was scared of giving up drink. I was scared of what I would feel in the evening without the comfort of alcohol. What would I do with myself, I couldn't just keep going for endless walks? I couldn't send my brain to sleep with TV because I didn't have one at the cottage (and was consequently in a constant battle with the TV licencing authority). How would I sleep if I hadn't numbed my brain before going to bed? Would I be fretting and shaking like I had been when I gave up smoking? After a lifetime of having an alcohol comfort blanket it was all too alien to contemplate. How would I cope every day for the rest of my life desperately wanting a drink and not being able to have one? I also worried about what my friends would think if I suddenly stopped drinking. Would they disown me? Would I end up envying and hating them?

It is interesting that of all the things I took into consideration when I contemplated giving up alcohol, I never thought of any of the positive aspects that would result. I never thought yippee I am going to be healthy and wonderfully fit and live for an extra twenty or thirty years. I never thought of all the money I would save. I never thought of all the pleasure I would bring to those I loved. I only ever focused on what I thought I would miss from drinking. Why is that? Is life without drink so <u>very</u> hard to imagine?

Question:

Before we go any further, what aspects of your life do you think would change if you were to quit alcohol as of tomorrow morning?

How many of those changes you have come up with are positive?

Then one day my wife and I went to my eldest Daughter's graduation at UCL. Not having been to university myself and not having had any involvement in further education I found the experience quite daunting, especially seeing all the dons and all the graduands in their caps and gowns, but as I proudly watched my daughter walk across the stage and shake hands with the dean as she collected her degree something in me snapped.

'I can do that!' I boldly said to my wife and later to my daughter, and they both gave me their 'heard it all before' look which I wholly deserved. But I was not to be put off.

By degrees

The one university I had heard of and was loosely familiar with from watching old TV programmes when I used to bunk off school was the Open University. Upon investigation it appeared that even without any qualifications worth speaking of, I could join a course and even take a whole degree if I wanted, but that I would have to do the entire thing from scratch and would be allowed no dispensation for having a related A' level or similar prior qualification. I decided to give the science starter course a try and see where it took me.

Within a few weeks the first book arrived, there would be twelve in all even for this basic level course, and I was allotted a tutor and given my first assignment to complete. The first book was called *Water for life* and proved to be fascinating. Instead of spending the time commuting to London idly staring out of the window, or sitting drunk on the way home I would study my book and found to my surprise I was loving learning after all these years. When I got my first assignment back and learnt I had passed and scored 95% I was completely hooked. The studying didn't stop me drinking at lunchtimes but it certainly made me cut back, and even in the evening I would get some coursework done before I hit the bottle.

A year later I had completed level one of a science degree course and signed up for year two, having decided to specialise in geosciences.

Two years later I had passed all my level two courses and had embarked on the two-year level three part of the course which would lead to the degree. By this time many of my previously scorn-full and disbelieving work colleagues knew I was going to see things through to the end, and many of them wished they had signed up at the same time as me. Because I had such a head start however, none of them did follow suit, more's the pity for them.

By now my family knew I was going to get my degree and the support I received was fantastic. I had also met loads of new people through the course, especially on the residential weeks away spent rock-hunting across Britain, and I had even met and got to know some famous scientists regularly to be seen on television, especially *The Sky at Night.*

Despite still drinking I was managing to cope with studying and with work, but only just. I talk some more about my work life in the next chapter. It was also half way through my degree course that my mother died from alcohol related liver failure which came to me as a complete shock. I knew Mum was getting frail in her old age, but it was only when I picked up her death certificate and saw the cause of death I realised and then discovered what had been going on, and that she had secretly been drinking bottles of vodka with my brother for months. And then a year later Paul went the same way. Living alone at the cottage during the week, commuting to the City most days to earn enough to pay the bills, studying as hard as I could, and being an alcoholic to boot, it is probably easy to understand why taking on the role of mentoring my brother and trying to keep him away from the bottle was never going to happen.

Despite all this, at the end of five years I walked across the stage and was awarded my degree by the Chancellor of the Open University, the film director David Puttnam.

A year later after completing a thesis on the 'likelihood and impact of an earthquake at Istanbul', I was awarded my honours and a 2.1.

To say I was delighted with myself and proud of myself would be an understatement. I had actually started **and** finished something, a rarity for me. I had achieved one of those dreams I had spent long wistful nights thinking about. I had found new interests including geology, astronomy and had some new firm friends, and I had intellectually grown. I knew how to read and write a scientific paper, how to analyse things better than I had ever done before, and I could apply all these new skills in both my work and home environments.

But I was still drinking far too much, and my health was beginning to suffer. The garden path edging was getting ever longer and we were even contemplating building a bottle tower tall enough to sit inside!

I was 52, my greatest ambition was to live longer than my brother had. He died age 56 - that gave me another four or five years to live, and if this sounds an incredible attitude to life to have, it shows how debilitated by alcohol I had become, and how old I felt at the time.

I deliberately repeat the above boxed statement. I was **52 years old**, and without realising it was because of the drink, I really felt my age. My greatest ambition was to live longer than my brother had. He died age 56 - that gave me another **four or five years to live**, and if this sounds an incredible attitude to life to have, it shows how debilitated by alcohol I had become, and how old I felt at the time.

Work life

When I had come back to the UK after my African adventure, I picked up on the insurance experience I had had in Johannesburg and got a job working for an insurance broker in the City. It helped that my father was one of the senior managers at the company otherwise I was probably unemployable in the UK at that stage of my life, and my elder brother had jumped on the same bandwagon and was working for the same company.

Somehow I had chosen an industry that had, and still has a massive drinking culture, and that of course suited me down to the ground. At the time I was twenty-five years old, I was married for the second time (that one didn't last long either) and I had a baby daughter.

Even on my first day at work I remember being taken to lunch by my new colleagues and getting drunk, not as some sort of initiation test, but purely because that's what they did most days. In the evening I would get the train home with my brother who at the time lived in the same road as me, and we would drink cider on the train and play the card game *spoof* with other City-based commuters similarly partial to drinking on the journey home. Sometimes we were so smashed we would take our own lives into our hands. The following story is an extract from my book 'The 7.52 to London Bridge' and provides a very graphic example!

A story - Extremely naughty boys

Although my brother and I lived in the same road and caught the same train each morning from Horley, we were not on speaking terms due to differences between our respective wives, and their cognisance of the fact that whenever my brother and I were together, it would end in mayhem. We would even stand on opposite ends of the station platform.

By evening however, the relationship had generally changed. For some reason, either one or both of us would have had a memorable luncheon involving such romanticised friends as Comrade Smirnoff,

General Gordon or Monsieur Chardonnay, and would need assistance back to London Bridge station to prepare for the journey homewards. Sometimes these lunches involved so many friends and comrades that an afternoon escape was in order. Fortunately the company we worked for wisely utilised large revolving electronic filing systems called 'Lektrievers'. These were ceiling height, about two metres wide and consisted of a series of double ranked shelves of coffin size that revolved waterwheel fashion when the shelf you required was dialled up on the keypad. Files were kept on these shelves in strict alphabetic order and to be frank it was an efficient system. To be even more frank it was a great place to be hidden if you were so drunk you needed to be kept away from management for the afternoon. Kind work-mates would lay you down on a rarely used shelf e.g. closed claim files S-Z, then send you to the back of the machine for a well-earned nap. This did take some getting used to, for if you woke up and panicked it was literally like having been buried alive and there was no escape until someone came to your rescue. If you were genuinely trying to work however, and urgently needed a file, it was particularly disconcerting as you waited for your selected shelf to arrive, to see seemingly dead colleagues rise from the depths and pass upwards as if on their way to that great wine bar in the sky.

As with most large City-based insurance companies, there were of course some unofficial ground rules you

were expected to follow and which were drummed
into you on your first day. At my company these
included:-

Rule 1

Try not to go back to the office if you have had six pints of
bitter, two bottles of red wine, a glass of port and a large gin
to drink at lunchtime. Most especially try and avoid going back
for a late afternoon important meeting with grumpy senior members
of staff who have no sense of humour.

Rule 2

If you need a new pencil or biro, do not waste time dealing with
the boring old fart in charge of stationary who will demand to
see a pencil stub or empty biro tube. Wait until after hours,
then rip the locked door off the stationary cupboard and help
yourself and your friends to anything you want, filling your
pockets if possible - but leave a polite thank-you note for the
old fart to treasure.

Rule 3

If you are dealing with an important and complex insurance claim
worth many thousands of pounds - you are completely out of your
depth, beginning to get stressed, and don't want to let on you
have effectively achieved nothing for the past two months - throw
the claims file off London Bridge into the Thames on your way to
the station on a Friday evening. Then have a wonderfully relaxed
weekend.

Rule 4

If you have been asked to leave the company for any reason
possibly associated with any of the above rules, don't forget to
throw ALL your important work off London Bridge into the Thames
on your way home.

As my brother was older than me and therefore had a
larger expense account, many afternoons I would be
called upon to dial him up and get him out of the
building before he could realise his full potential for
havoc. We would somehow tumble our way across
London Bridge to London Bridge station, find our

waiting train and of course, enter the buffet car where the ever smiling buffet attendant was ready to introduce us to new liquid friends. If we missed the train, London Bridge station had a wonderful buffet of its own, staffed by large and jolly beaming-faced West Indian ladies. Somehow they knew exactly how to make a pink gin (you throw out the angostura bitters) and a couple of these would steady us nicely for the journey home. Pink gin had become a favourite as both my brother and I had joined the Territorial Army, had been somehow identified as being potential officers and consequently reinvented ourselves as such, revelling in all the pomp and show.

Once aboard the train and suitably fuelled, we would work our way down the wonderful corridor carriages, and find somewhere appropriately concealed to lounge, lizard style.

Even though these were twelve coach trains, they were made up of three sets of four carriages, each of which had a driver's cab at each end. Quite by chance it so happened that a Chubb door key used correctly could open the locks to these cabs. Inside could be found two convenient and comfortable revolving seats; a dash board consisting of interesting and irresistible knobs and switches; and a couple of shelves of useful goodies such as explosive charges for use on the track to stop other trains in fog if there was an emergency. These latter items could be detonated by throwing a brick at them and were powerful enough to do considerable damage - apparently. Although you couldn't go into the front cab of course because the real driver was in there, or indeed the rear cab where the guard was usually based, you could turn the train lights on and off; blow the horn lots and lots of times; and say 'hello' to the driver and guard through the intercom – which always came as a bit of a shock to them both. Whilst the guard was running in a mad panic through the train to find which cab we were in and stop our fun, we would exit our cab, stand nicely and innocently in our smart business suits until he/she went by, then go to the now empty cab at the rear of the train, where we had the additional advantage of a rear view as we sped on our journey, hooting the horn for all it was worth. To avoid having our enjoyment curtailed, where the sets of four carriages joined there was a big heavy yellow door which was opened inwards to create a passageway thereby making up a longer train, or closed tightly shut and bolted if this was the front or rear cab. Once past the guard we could close one of these yellow doors behind us trapping the guard in the front part of the train and cutting off the guard's route through to us. What fun to sit glass in hand, watching the parallel lines of the track disappear to a distant point, and seeing all the interesting railway paraphernalia race past.

Just once, we were in just such a situation on a very wintry Christmas Eve having spent the afternoon celebrating in a wine bar, and we decided the rearward view, although spectacular with snow drifting across the tracks, was insufficient reward for such a festive occasion. We therefore opened the big rear yellow door of the train.

At the time we were probably travelling at about 90 mph and as we struggled to pull the heavy door inwards, the icy wind plucked hard at our clothes. The noise of the train became one long roar as the wheels thundered over the rails which narrowed away from us into the distant twilight. And, as complete idiots do, we dared each other to step outside. Above the train buffers and the central coupling there was a narrow ledge just wide enough to get half a step on, but all there was to hold on to was a grime-smeared vacuum pipe and a small metal hand rail, itself held on by two small loose screws. Above these however and at head height, was a sturdy looking window wiper on either side of the doorway, so gripping onto these we both somehow managed to manoeuvre ourselves outside, swivel round to face the rear, and ended up each sitting astride a massive buffer. Clutching with all our might onto the vacuum pipes and metal handrails behind us, we both sat in this death defying position, kicking our legs in thin air just above the level of the tracks. We looked at each other in disbelief and I know the madness I felt was fully reflected in my brother's eyes. Then we started screaming, both with exhilaration, and sheer terror at what we were doing.

Very soon the train tore through Purley station where we could see startled and alarmed station staff pointing at us and yelling, then the train hit some sets of points which shook it from side to side and made my teeth rattle in my head. By now I felt completely sober, massively dehydrated and sick with fear. I knew I was literally inches from death and as stuck in my position as the proverbial kid with his 'head through the railings'. If anything, the train seemed to have sped up and the track and the trees to the side were passing in a blur.

The train thundered into a railway cutting with towering walls on either side, shutting out what little light there had been, and casting a deep gloom over the snow-laden scene. Despite being frozen to the marrow, I was sweating profusely and beginning to really panic. I was losing my grip on the vacuum pipe and had visions of the screws working their way loose on the handrail. I saw my brother turn to look at me and could tell he was in a similar petrified state. This was no longer fun and I wished so hard it was all a dream.

The walls of the cutting grew even higher and seemed to meet overhead making me feel insignificant and very vulnerable. Now the train raced past a long disused signal-box, the sole sentinel before the mouth of the mile long Merstham tunnel. If ever there was a sight to conjure up Dickensian ghosts from a Christmas past, it was that lonely and long forgotten signal-box, somehow lit as if from within by a last failing ray of winter sun – I could even imagine a spectral voice from the roof of the cutting calling 'Helloa, below there!' I know I had tears in my eyes.

The cacophony of noise became deafening as we entered the pitch blackness of the tunnel, I stared mesmerised as the entrance to the tunnel reduced to a tiny dot and then disappeared before my eyes. The steel wheels on the steel rails screamed as we rattled and shook; sparks sprayed from beneath the train illuminating the shiny track in an orange hue. Occasionally there would be an explosion of electric blue sparks from the third rail – the scaring conductor rail which carries the power. When this happened the tunnel would be lit for a split-instant creating monstrous shadows, and tainting the air with a thick metallic burning smell on top of the damp sooty aroma left over from a century of steam trains. After less than a minute of this overpowering, mind-numbing experience we had both had enough, this was the stuff supposed to be reserved for nightmares. The freezing buffers were slippery with thick grease, we were numb with cold, our arms ached from holding on for dear life, and we had both had visions of the big yellow door slamming shut and leaving us trapped outside to a hideous fate. Even worse was the thought that a train would come the other way, tear past our train with only inches to spare, and suck us off our precarious perch either to be cut to pieces under the wheels, or skinned alive and torn to ribbons as we were dragged dangling behind. But somehow - I will never know how, we were suddenly back in the warm rear cab with its friendly subdued glow of light, the big yellow door was slammed shut against the horror outside, and we stood staring at each other and then hugging each other with relief.

Without needing to say anything, we both walked as far up the train to the front as possible (remember, we had closed off half the train to shut out the guard), and tidied ourselves up as best we could as the train slowed down for Horley station.

Obviously the onlookers at Purley had passed the word, and at Horley the train was met by the station master, a few more station staff, and lots of Police. As we had expected however, they were grouped at the back of the train ready to pounce on and arrest two young idiot hooligans. The last people they suspected were two serious looking, smartly dressed, pin-striped businessmen, alighting from the train a few carriages from the rear, and thankfully with thick black winter coats hiding the mass of grease on their nice suit trousers which inevitably ended up in the dustbin. Only the young yob-like ticket inspector (who recognised a drunk when he saw one), grinned knowingly at us and chuckled to himself as we passed out of the station. After all – It was Christmas. And at home, I had waiting for me my very first little daughter, who would be waking up the next morning to open her own, very first little train-set, from Santa.

And, if she was really lucky, she could even watch me play with it in complete safety!

Question:

What is the most stupid and dangerous thing you have done when drunk?

What is the most stupid and dangerous thing you have done sober?

Probably before just as had happened at school I was once again 'asked to leave', I exited the business side of the insurance industry and became involved in sales of computer software technology to that same industry. This was great fun, I seemed to be very good at it and within a few years I was the owner of my own small but successful software company. The key to my popularity with clients and prospects alike was my provision of regular and generous lunches, especially in the wine department, and many a deal I actually closed purely because of my ability to out-drink someone, especially when dealing with the Eastern Europeans. Most of my sales however were to City of London based insurance operations, and through people I had met and got to know during my time on the business side. The City really is a place where 'who you know' counts far more than what you know.

Despite the company doing well, being the owner and Managing Director of the company there were no controls on my behaviour or my expenditure. My drinking therefore got out of hand, and some lunchtimes I was so drunk my wife who also worked for me would either have to help me home, or go looking for me by trawling around the many wine bars I was known to frequent. Once she found me sitting on a pile of bricks in a building site, completely flummoxed as to where I was and what time it was. As an author, I have now turned many of these experiences into a set of amusing tales in my latest book of memoirs. It was a blessing that before I could do any long-term damage to my company it was eventually purchased by a larger enterprise and I was set free to start a new venture.

In the intervening years up to and then after I started my degree, I had been involved in a number of enterprises, some successful, some less so and my life still revolved around the London Insurance Market based in the City. I had set myself up as a self-employed consultant, and drink played so much a part of my daily business routine, taking a cue from my scientific reading I even used the chemical formula for ethanol as my business logo. In fact it still is!

jkpartnership

ideas and innovation in sales

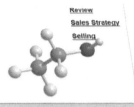

Every day would involve meeting friends and contacts in a wine bar at lunch time, and most days that's where the afternoon hours were spent as well. Many of the people I associated with were of a similar age to me and also had a liking for excessive amounts of alcohol. Many of them were also suffering the effects of a life spent drinking and like me, were feeling every year of their age. It is hardly surprising in this environment that to live until your mid-sixties was considered a good innings.

But I was fast becoming tired of the old routine and I needed a change. Having the degree and all that new learning had awakened ambition and a thirst for knowledge within me, and I suppose I knew in a way the drink was slowly killing me (my wife certainly knew because as I will allude to later in this book, she was already making provision for the fact I would not be around forever) but having been self-employed for so long I didn't have the luxury of a fat pension I could take early retirement on and just enjoy studying. It was time to find something new, and as luck had it, it came my way sooner than I expected.

Back to School

It is hard to laugh and smile all the time when you are feeling ill and in pain, and it makes you feel **old**. I felt **old**, and that made me **old**, and gave me an **old** outlook on life.

When you feel old and consequently act as if old age is upon you, you don't expect to change career and open up a fresh chapter in your life. Instead you think you know what awaits you. I had already made the mental decision I didn't want to end up in some care home or being pushed around in a wheelchair having made myself decrepit through misuse of my own body. I also knew that my wife would be cared for if I died before state retirement age as I had long before taken out some life insurance. The reason I felt so old was mainly down to gout. Gout can have many causes, which offer the alcoholic a similar number of excuses for avoiding the most likely cause, drink. I knew deep down my gout was as a result of drink, but I hung on to the genetically inherited excuse (my mother and brother both had gout – but then they were also both alcoholics), the too much red meat excuse (although I didn't eat red meat – only pork), and the allergic to various foodstuffs excuse (although I only ever ate the same bland meals).

I was so used to having gout I would only notice it when it was really bad to the extent I couldn't walk properly, or the pain became too much to bear. The rest of the time I was suffering a constant background pain or I had swollen knees or ankles. For years I had been unable to kneel down properly, to climb ladders to help decorate, to run, to cycle easily, or to do many things I now take for granted. The only time I really felt free from the gout was when I was too drunk to be aware of anything. It is hard to laugh and smile all the time when you are feeling ill and in pain, and it makes you feel old. I felt old, and that made me old, and gave me an old outlook on life.

But then an opportunity came my way.

The Open University wrote to me and invited me to join their Student Associate Scheme to see if having graduated with a science degree I might like to explore becoming a teacher. I could hardly believe it.

I called the university the next day and they told me all I had to do was find a local school that would let me go and spend three weeks with them. The university would send me a programme of work to complete during the three weeks, and at the end of the session if I wanted to become a teacher and assuming the work I sent in was of a sufficient standard they would help me become a real bona fide teacher. On top of this they would pay me a few hundred pounds for the trouble.

Having completed my degree I was missing having a challenge and I was so used to having to spend my spare time studying this new challenge couldn't have arrived at a better time.

To cut a long story short, I completed the student associate scheme, I loved every second of the three weeks spent in a secondary school, and I decided despite being in my mid-fifties to go back to school and become a teacher. In the three week period I had even stopped drinking during the day (there was no way I was going to go anywhere near mixing booze and working with schoolchildren), and I felt younger and more enthused than I had for years.

The one drawback was money. To become a teacher I would have to do a one year course during which all I would receive was a small bursary, and following that I would be on teacher pay for many years. Far less than I was used to earning in the City. The only solution was to sell our two homes, and buy one new home thus halving our monthly bills and releasing enough capital to see us through for a few years. Within a few short months we had carried this plan through to completion, we were living by the sea on the South coast of England and I had started a PGCE course at the local university.

School and drink don't mix

The wonderful thing about doing the PGCE is it took me away from the City and allowed me to break with routine. The bad thing is it didn't stop me drinking!

Teaching naturally involves children and I had promised to myself not to touch a drop of alcohol during the school day or whenever I was around children, and I am proud to report I stuck rigidly to my resolve. Even when asked to accompany and help out on a three day school trip to the Isle of Wight for eleven-year-olds, I didn't touch a drop of booze. On this little adventure we were all staying in various large boarding houses across the island, and the house I was in accommodated about fifty children and four adult teachers of which I was one. After the kids were finally in bed the two female teachers also turned in for the night, but myself and the other male teacher stayed awake and sat in the kitchen in case any children got scared or had other issues. The other chap had some beers he had brought with him and I drank tea. I didn't do this to show off or curry favour but because I knew if I had one drink I would want lots to drink, so the only way to cope was to have nothing, and actually because of the circumstances and the huge responsibility I felt it didn't bother me at all. (To be honest I was more concerned about waking the whole house up with my record-braking snoring once I finally went to bed – something that is not quite as bad since I stopped drinking, but don't expect any miracle snoring cure!)

Unfortunately, for the rest of the time I was doing the PGCE, once school was over and I arrived home the first thing I would do is 'celebrate' my day by downing a glass of wine.

'That's another day where I haven't had a boozy lunch!' I would say to my wife, and I genuinely felt proud of myself. But then it would all go rapidly downhill.

Any of you reading this who has also undertaken teacher training will know it involves a phenomenal amount of paperwork, home study and report writing. On top of this, a couple of weeks into the course you actually commence teaching your own classes and so you have lesson planning to contend with. At this stage of your development a one hour lesson might take well over one hour to plan (and I was teaching science), so if you are teaching an average of three lessons per day that is a lot of after school work to allow for.

I would have my glass of wine, set out my work programme for the evening and then stupidly have another glass of wine.

I might plan the easiest lesson first, then have another glass. Then plan a further lesson and down a further glass.

My wife would call me for dinner which would involve more wine, I would half-heartedly do some paperwork over yet more wine, and then I might go for a walk to try and sober up a little and clear my head after which I would promise to myself I would put the most complex lesson plan together. It never happened.

By the time I got round to planning the lesson I most needed to be sober for, I would be pissed and incapable of compiling anything other than drivel. I would pack up my things, set the alarm clock for five the following morning and instead do the planning when I woke up (tired and at less than my best). This led to a tired day, a tired teacher, and me being far less effective in class than would otherwise have been the case.

This self-induced stress filled lifestyle coupled with wine-filled evenings also led to my gout flaring up, but desperate not to miss a single day through illness I went to school regardless, and many a day I could be seen painfully limping around, especially If I was carrying a heavy box of books to take home and mark. I of course told everyone I had an old sports injury that had flared up. Wearing the pain on my face also made me look unhappy and anxious, and that in turn worried the other teachers who thought I might not be enjoying teaching, or that they were somehow doing something to upset me.

Question:

Do you suffer ill effects such as gout or severe headaches through drinking, and if so do you lie and pretend there is something else wrong with you?

Monday mornings were the worst because I would binge at the weekend to make up for the no lunches in the week. I would even put off the lesson planning for Monday's lessons until the very last thing on Sunday night. This meant it was never done properly and I would have to do it in the early hours of Monday morning either accompanied by a hangover, or still feeling pissed!

The great shame is I loved teaching, I was good at it and I loved being with the children, but it all became too much for me and with only one month of the course left to complete I jacked it in.

There are other issues that also came into play and that helped lead to my decision to quit and they may have made me leave anyway, but I do know one thing for sure: –

I would have given teaching a far better shot had I been the sober person I am now. I would have been far fitter, far healthier, had much more energy, had more time, been more organised, been much more relaxed and had my wits about me to a far greater extent.

A complete re-think

I left off being a student teacher and returned to the City. Naturally, the very first day I was back to my old ways and getting smashed at lunchtime but somehow it didn't feel quite the same. I no longer enjoyed the commuting, the getting home late and being back in the same old routine as before. I had seen a glimpse of an alternative lifestyle and it had started me thinking.

On top of this, in our new home by the sea I was meeting a lot of people far older than myself, many in their late seventies or early eighties, the sort of folks I had previously imagined would be in an old folk's home at their advanced age. But instead, these guys were fit and active and even pushing heavy boats up and down the beach. In the City most of the 'older' people I knew or had been associated with were in their early sixties, had already taken early retirement or were now dead. I had never contemplated living much past retirement age and as you already know, since my brother's death I had considered living longer than he had lasted to be a fair timespan for someone with my lifestyle.

Now I was mixing with these old men and **all** of them acted younger and were fitter than me. Sometimes they would ask me to help launch a boat and I had to pretend I was nursing that fake sports injury, or I would go for a walk (limp) with my wife and make sure they weren't around at the time so I wouldn't be embarrassed as I hobbled by. I hated it and I hated being unfit and unwell. I genuinely envied them their health and the extra years they had over me. I mentally blamed them for not having to have spent their lives working in the City with all that supposed stress, but it turns out that many of them had had far more stressful jobs than me, and some had even been war heroes. But I was blinkered to that. I hated everything and I hated what I was.

But it didn't stop me drinking!

As well as the regular bouts of gout, I also had high blood pressure and was taking tablets for that. I also had high cholesterol and was taking tablets for that. I had been diagnosed with type 2 diabetes and was having regular check-ups for that. In fact I was falling apart and I hated it too.

But it didn't stop me drinking!

Even though we hadn't been in our new house that long my wife was unhappy with it and was suggesting we should move again. The house was too big, it was too remote from the places she knew and too remote from her friends and family.

What I couldn't see because I didn't want to see it at the time was that she didn't expect me to live that much longer, and she wanted to move back to somewhere she would feel safe and secure before I died. How bloody terrible is that! How awful that she had to live with someone she loved who was selfishly drinking themselves to an early grave!

Question:

Have you ever considered what your loved ones may really think about what you are doing to yourself, and whether they worry what will happen to them if you fall hopelessly ill or die?

But it didn't stop me drinking!

At Christmas the gout came back with such vengeance I could hardly get out of bed or move my legs without being in agony. The previous day I had had a friend round and got hopelessly drunk, polishing off bottle after bottle of different types of wine (typical Christmas selection), some spirits and even some home-made sloe gin. As usual I hadn't had any water to drink with any of it and so had ended up massively dehydrated.

That following morning I sat alone upstairs and decided enough was enough. I was going to stop drinking forever. No half measures, I knew they wouldn't work with me, I was simply going to stop drinking. I didn't want to wait until New Year as an excuse to give up then as so many do for Dry January, I just decided then and there **never ever to touch alcohol again**.

And I have never touched a drop since!

I didn't consider or even care what living without alcohol would be like, I just knew it had to be better than what I was experiencing, and I of course had no inkling of the fabulous new life that awaited me.

I didn't consider getting any outside assistance because I was in too much of a hurry to start not drinking and in any case I wouldn't have known where to turn that suited me. In the past I had half-heartedly glanced through alcoholism self-help books in a local book shop in the City (I think I was seeking reassurance that I wasn't an alcoholic) but the ones I looked at all seemed to be academic and text book in style. They also appeared to focus on the negative health aspects of alcohol which of course I already knew about. I also didn't want to join any groups because of what my brother had experienced at rehab, and because of what I had heard of the religious style groups that definitely weren't for me. (Incidentally I don't knock these groups at all, but as I say, they just weren't for me.)

Instead I sat in my bedroom and devised my own focused methodology loosely based around the method I had used to successfully quit smoking some twenty years earlier. I wrote it down, I determined to follow it come what may and it worked. I started my new regime that same day and I have never looked back.

I have to admit I didn't expect things to be easy. Towards the end of this book I talk about what that very first day was really like.

How wedded was I to alcohol?

In my book 'I Don't Drink!' I ask myself if I was an alcoholic and conclude that yes I was. I arrive at this outcome by asking myself a series of questions such as did I drink first thing in the morning, did I drink every day, did I tank up or binge drink, did I physically feel I needed a drink, and did I ever plan my day around drink (not all of which I answered yes too I hasten to add). There is a video on my website you can watch, and through which you can take the quiz yourself if you feel so inclined. **It's called the alcoholic truth quiz.**

www.idontdrink.net/videos

Whilst I was drinking however, I never considered myself to be an alcoholic. I had a clear vision of how an alcoholic looked and behaved and I certainly didn't fit that bill, but my brother did. Towards the end of his life he looked gaunt and shrivelled and had yellowing skin and eyes, but even before that he was showing signs of being physically worn out as if he was twenty years my senior not five. He was also apparently drinking a bottle of wine at breakfast time just to kick-start the day, and whenever I saw him we would have to stop at every bar we passed just so he could have yet another vodka to keep him going. That in my mind was what an alcoholic was like, and I wasn't like that at all. What told me that I was an alcoholic, was realising and admitting to myself that for as many years as I could remember I had been planning every single day around drink.

Question:

If I ask you to draw a tick every time you think about drink in the course of a day, how many ticks will you make?

I would start with a tick when I woke up. Either because I would be wishing I hadn't had so much to drink the night before, or because I would already be planning when I was going to have my first drink that day. I would mentally compartmentalise the next twenty-four hours into measured slots. Go to work; organise who to meet for lunch and drinks; do some work; go to lunch; go back to the office and do some work; go home and relax with some drink.

I would at the same time establish in my mind how much drink I had available to me so I could plan to buy more if necessary. (It is amazing that of all the things I would forget, somehow I always knew how much booze was in the house.)

If it was a weekend and we were going out in the evening I would try and plan to go out early and offer to drive, knowing I could convince my wife to drive home meaning I could drink. Going early of course meant I could drink earlier.

All of the above thought processes would happen even as I was getting out of bed.

As the day wore on I would be measuring myself against how my drinking plan was going, even without consciously doing so. I remember I would think things like 'I haven't had that much to drink this lunchtime because of that meeting I had to get back for, and therefore the two-thirds of a bottle of wine at home won't be enough. I will need to buy an extra bottle on the way home.'

If I was due to meet someone I would try and plan it that we could either meet or end up in a wine bar.

If I was due to have lunch with someone I didn't know, or who I knew didn't drink much, I would think of which colleague or friend I could invite along who would also drink, so I could still drink lots of wine and not come across as a lush. There is nothing worse than drinking a whole bottle of wine over lunch when you are with someone who is only having water. It's even worse if the conversation is still going strong and you feel the need to order a second bottle and they are **still** on bloody water! I know because I been there and done that countless times!

If my wife or someone suggested we go out for the day or to visit somewhere, which could be anywhere, I would think 'that will be nice, I am sure there will be somewhere there where I can have a drink.'

If I read a holiday brochure and it showed pictures of a nice beach I would scan the picture looking for the bar or think 'that will be a nice place to sit and have a drink'.

If I heard some music it would often bring a drink to mind.

If I saw a billboard advertising drink I would be able to taste it!

> **The mental plan for my whole day revolved around drink – everyday!**

Question:

How soon after you wake up do you think about drink?

Challenge:

Carry a ballpoint pen with you, and try stopping yourself and making a tick on your wrist every time you let drink dictate any element of your day. This might be adjusting the time you do something, or something you put off because you wouldn't be able to have a drink. If you get at least one tick then drink is influencing and even dictating your day.

Challenge:

Now actually try ticking your wrist every time you think about drink or having a drink. If you get more than a dozen ticks that should really be telling you something.

I never tried this challenge when I was drinking because no-one suggested it to me, but I know I would have lost miserably and had a huge number of ticks on my wrist. How do I know this?

I know it because of the immense freedom I feel now I don't drink. The 'something's missing' feeling I got when I first went sober was quite peculiar. I would even ask my wife if there was something I had promised to do but hadn't done, it just felt so strange not having that nagging 'you need a drink' devil prodding me all the time. It was like a mental list of negative thoughts had disappeared. Here is an example of the sort of thing I mean based on a simple request from my wife:-

> Shall we go to London tomorrow? We haven't been to town for ages and we could see a show, have dinner and get the late train back?

Past thoughts

- I had planned on having a relaxing afternoon at home, watching a war film and drinking that nice Sancerre in the fridge
- It's a long train journey and unlike when I'm on my own I won't be able to drink with her there.
- I like the idea of a show and dinner in London but someone has to drive home from the station when we get back. I can't ask her as it would be such a rare treat for her to have a glass of champagne at the theatre.
- I will have to cope with going to the bar at the show and not ordering a drink.
- I will have to cope with dinner after the show and drinking water.
- I will have to cope with not drinking on the train home.
- When we get home it will be too late to then have loads of wine even though I know I will be desperate.
- Arrgghh – but I will have to say yes and pretend to enjoy myself. Why oh why did she have to suggest this?

New thoughts

- What a great idea, I will enjoy her being able to have some champagne, and on the way home from the station we can have the top down and go for a nice starlit drive listening to some Fleetwood Mac. We could even have a late coffee on the beach if the café at Wittering is still open.

If the above sounds contrived I can assure you it isn't. It is the same with every aspect of my life now. Drink simply doesn't feature and therefore it can't get in the way and interfere.

Question:

What thought processes might go through your head given a similar style request from your partner?

Being possessive about alcohol

I have put this section in under how wedded I was to alcohol because in many ways I might as well have been married to the stuff!

Question:

Do you ever get possessive about 'your' drink?

I did, and quite often. If I was out for dinner with friends I would worry about who was drinking what. What particularly concerned me was no-one saying they wanted anything alcoholic to drink and then when the bottle of wine I had ordered for myself arrived, they all decide to have a glass of that anyway. That used to drive me crazy. I used to reluctantly pour them as small amount as I thought I could get away with so as to keep as much for myself. I also used to stand the bottle next to me like I owned it, and to stop anyone else helping themselves.

What I hated most of all were situations like that just described, which inevitably led to me only having one glass, but when I then ordered a further bottle the others would look disapprovingly at me as though I was an alcoholic (which of course I was, but that was my business not theirs).

If guests visited our house I would often keep the nice wine for myself and give them cheap muck.

If we were low on drink and we had people visiting, I would have a secret bottle hidden in the kitchen so I could pop out and keep my own drinking going without the risk of completely running out of booze early in the evening, or me having to go without.

Sometimes, even if we had lots of alcohol in the house, I would have a secret bottle on the go just so people wouldn't see how much I really did drink.

Question:

Have you ever maintained a secret bottle of drink just to hide your drinking from others?

People's attitudes – a big reason for <u>not</u> stopping drinking?

People who don't drink are idiots!

When I was a drinker I made a deliberate point of avoiding anyone who didn't drink, especially from a work perspective. I know that many of my work colleagues who still drink do the same and many of them (without saying anything) probably try and avoid me if they can:

'Oh blast here's bloody Julian coming through the door. Now I expect all we will hear is how fit and healthy he is; we will have to say how well he looks; and we can't have a good laugh and get pissed until he clears off again.'

'I'm planning a corporate day out but I won't invite Julian, he doesn't drink. It wouldn't do to have anyone like that spoiling a good day out.'

People who don't drink always instilled unwanted or unwarranted emotions and attitudes in me:

Guilt. They were doing something I couldn't do and that I knew I hadn't even tried doing. I would imagine them going home to a happy household and a contented wife and knew that by comparison I had created a monster best kept under wraps.

Assumption. I knew they would be boring people with nothing funny to share and that most of their life would involve reading, walking and doing gentle things that involved no risk. By comparison I saw myself as someone always up for anything, prepared to give 'it' a go, a real 'no holds barred' individual.

Inferiority. Perhaps through the guilt aspect of my emotions I would feel like a naughty boy to these people with them taking on a superior teacher or parental status in my mind.

Suspicion. Could I trust someone who didn't drink? Would they be listening to and taking in every word I spoke whilst I wouldn't remember what I had said, or even worse would I say things I shouldn't once I had had a few drinks? Surely better to be with people who are all going to be drunk than take the risk of having a potential spy in our midst.

Envy? I didn't ever envy the lifestyle of these non-drinking idiots, after all I didn't want to stop drinking so what was there to be envious about. Sometimes however, late in the evening I would still be in a wine bar, I would know I was going to get home really late and in a drunken state, and I would envy someone I might have been with earlier who was sober, and would already be home having fun with their family. **I would envy them a great deal then.**

I would envy them a great deal the next morning if I woke with a hangover or a splitting headache, just knowing they were having a healthy guilt-free weekend and that I had already ruined the start of mine.

Question:

What do you think of the sober people you know (assuming you know some), especially those who have given up drinking?

How fair is your opinion of them? And is any of that opinion driven by a secret wish to be the same but continuing to have as much fun as you are having now?

Does your attitude and your opinion of sober people put you off quitting, it did me?

Have you ever met anyone who has told you they are a teetotaller?

The one type of person I never met was anyone who outwardly referred to themselves as 'teetotal'. Had I done so I would probably have run a mile, expecting otherwise to be roped into joining their sect, or classed as a sinner and banished to the alcohol fuelled fires of hell. To me, there really is something so negative about this teetotal label and it's one of the reasons I suggest avoiding the usage of the moniker in 'I Don't Drink!' I truly expect to see teetotallers going around handing out leaflets and accompanied by someone playing a tambourine.

On the subject of teetotallers, Wikipedia states:

The teetotalism movement was first started in Preston England, in the early 19th century. The Preston Temperance Society was founded in 1833 by Joseph Livesey who was to become a leader of the temperance movement and the author of *The Pledge*: "We agree to abstain from all liquors of an intoxicating quality whether ale, porter, wine or ardent spirits, except as medicine."

Authors note: I had a Great Uncle Percy, a Methodist who was heavily influenced by the temperance movement. He was always drinking something medicinal from a secret bottle he kept hidden about his person. He also suffered from gout!

So just because I don't drink it doesn't make me 'weird' or 'strange' or 'queer' as my mother would say, but how you introduce and put yourself across to others once you quit alcohol is important.

But what do people think of YOU now?

I now know people were avoiding having lunch with me or meeting with me in the afternoon. Since giving up I have been told on numerous occasions how people I thought liked me and wanted to do business with me wrote me off as a drunk after mid-day. I know there are job opportunities I was considered for but then immediately dismissed as a candidate because I was seen as a drunk. No-one ever used the word alcoholic, I was just known as someone who drank too much.

Now I don't drink I see other people in that same light. There are friends I would not go and see after 2 p.m. because they will have had too much to drink, so any conversation with them would be meaningless or just a repeat of what they told me last time I saw them and which they will have forgotten they told me. It all sounds a bit cruel but that is the reality.

One for the road?

Now I realise I was often the driver for us all having too much to drink. I was the one forcing another bottle of wine on everyone and saying 'one for the road' over and over again. I was the bad news, I was the nightmare. I was the one about whom other people's wives would say 'Oh no, I hope you're not seeing Julian after work are you?'

Question:

What job opportunities might you have missed or be missing because you drink?

Do you think there might be people who avoid you or don't include you because you drink too much? Do you care? Really?

What about your mates in the local bar?

You might lose some friends if you give up drinking, some people just don't or don't want to understand. There might be people you have to upset and tell them you won't be seeing quite as much of them as before. You might not want to do that.

You might not get invited to that stag or hen night as a non-drinker, after all you might now be considered boring and not expected to join in the fun as much. But perhaps you could offer to be the driver for the evening and be a hero that way, and also make sure the others you are with are relatively safe and not likely to injure themselves because they are too drunk. But you might not want to do that either.

You might have the sort of friends my brother had.

He was mixing with the crowd you find in the pub at 11.00 in the morning, already on their second drink at least. He could relate to them because all conversation was either about the next drink or some repeated tale they had all heard countless times but would never remember. These were the 'friends' who broke my brother out of rehab so he could go drinking with them. The fact he had inherited money from our mum and was stupid enough to let everyone put their drinks on his bar tab might have had something to do with it. It also doesn't say much for the integrity of the pub manager that he allowed someone so obviously alcoholic to run a bar tab in the first instance, after all, being bright yellow with jaundice is a bit of a giveaway.

When you quit drinking some things have to change – and some people have to go!

Question:

Who would you see a lot less of and how much would that really matter?

You might find you make a whole lot of new friends, that you find new things to have in common, that knowing new people opens up a whole new world of interests for you, and that having more time for each other without an alcoholic bond results in far firmer friendships than you might ever have had. Of course it doesn't mean your new friends have to be non-drinkers as well, but you might find they drink in moderation which won't bother you at all, whereas if they are heavy drinkers you might find it will annoy you and frustrate you, it certainly does me.

You might even find more time to like yourself a whole lot more and be able to rely on your own company. You might even become your own best friend.

But some relationships you have to maintain and they might always have involved a lot of drink.

Strategic business partners, fellow club members and family members at annual gatherings fall into this category, I am sure there are more. These are the sort of people with whom you feel obliged to have a drink with because it will be expected of you. These are the sort of people who will keep saying 'go on, one glass won't hurt you' and similar unhelpful encouragements – the sort of person I was.

For these people you need to devise some good excuses, especially if you are unlikely to see them often and don't want to tell them you have quit alcohol until you have gone without for such a long time, they could put you on the rack and you still wouldn't back down and have a drink.

Some ideas for excuses:

Diving

Many years ago I was in Miami at a client of mine's corporate event. They had invited literally hundreds of their own clients and all their staff to a huge bash at a palatial hotel. It was so huge they had three bands playing at the same time, people in costume running food stalls and an endless sea of drink, especially champagne. I was wrecked that night but I remember very well talking to the company Finance Director and asking him why he wasn't also drinking and only had a glass of water.

'I am going night diving at 1 a.m.' he replied. 'The tuna hereabouts are in massive shoals at this time of year but they sleep at night, you can swim amongst them which is apparently amazing!'

It did sound amazing and I was amazed. I was also so impressed with the FD, as were most other people who had heard his story, that he became a hero that evening and anything but a pariah for not drinking. Only a complete moron would have expected him to have an alcoholic drink before going night diving.

Flying

Assuming you don't live in Miami or have a similar opportunity for night diving you could say you are having a flying lesson first thing the following morning. You certainly can't drink and fly, especially if you are in training and no-one would expect you to. It also makes you sound really interesting. If you want to really impress, how about a helicopter flying lesson?

Driving

Yes, you could say you are driving the next day and that should be good enough, but it probably isn't going to be. So many people will say 'just one will be OK' you will have to be quite forceful to get them to stop pushing you. A track day on the other hand would be different. Saying you are going to be flying round the track in a Ferrari the following morning is another matter altogether.

Illness or being on antibiotics?

Too boring unless unfortunately true.

Night kayaking

I have tried this excuse and it worked really well. I explained that a friend and I were going a mile offshore that night to see the Milky Way far away from any light pollution, that we were going to take snorkels and masks in case we saw any seals or porpoises, and that we would be offshore for at least two hours. Instead of being a boring sober idiot I became someone everyone wanted to talk to.

Romance

Whether you are married or single, male or female, simply explaining that you are going for a romantic drive that evening to 'see where it takes you', has to be an excuse everyone would understand.

The really great thing is you will feel so much fitter once you quit drinking and you will be saving so much money, there is no reason why ALL these excuses (not the illness) can't be true tales. And of course you WILL be SOBER so you CAN do them!

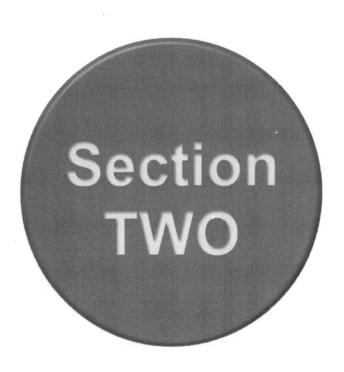

Section
TWO

A voyage of self-discovery

Let's now look at some specific aspects of everyday life and see how we can map them to what your day looks like. In this section I talk about work, play, health, and family and by using examples from my own experience try and tease out what might be affected by drink in your current life and how things might change for the better if you were to quit alcohol. There are no hard and fast rules here and no one size fits all solution. I am sure there will readers who will shout 'It's all right for him, I have this issue to contend with, or this illness, or no money, or whatever', but the idea is to get you to think through your daily life as a series of compartments and within each, try and explore how much of an impact the fact you drink is having. Try and answer the questions.

Work

Living over two hours commute away from London, I now work whenever I can from home and only make the trek to town for meetings or for a demonstration to a prospect. For the record I am a business development consultant for a software company based in the City. That title is a posh alternative to 'salesman', the sort of job where drinking and entertaining is viewed as being de rigueur. Because I'm spending far less money than I was when I was drinking I have also been able to cut down the amount of paid hours I work, and have achieved a work/life balance that is the envy of many of my friends and colleagues.

When I was drinking my working day unofficially finished at lunchtime after which I would be too pissed to achieve anything sensible. Now I can pick up and put down work at any time of the day. From March to October when the sea is kind enough, that might mean making some calls and writing up meeting notes in the morning for an hour or two, then going kayaking or for a swim in the sea, then some more telephoning, then a cycle ride, and then doing some writing for a new book. The time is mine, the work gets done, I enjoy it and everyone wins.

Although I never think about drink anymore, because I have been writing this book I **have** been thinking what my life used to be like. The other day I arrived very early in the City for a seminar which meant traversing London Bridge with the thousands of commuters who make that same drudging journey every day, just like I used to. I remembered the feeling of going into the office when I worked for other people, and knowing I had been out of order the day before. Perhaps I had been rude, or just too drunk, or I had been too obviously pissed in front of a customer, or had been too drunk to even dare risk going back to work in the afternoon. I remembered the awful stress-filled feeling of knowing I was going to be in serious trouble when I arrived in the office and possibly even sacked. I remembered feverishly thinking what I could say or lie about to try and save myself, and all the time wishing with all my heart I could turn the clock back and not have been drunk the day before. So many times I would think, 'if only.'

Even worse was if it was a **Monday** morning, the drinking episode had been on the Friday and I had ruined the weekend fretting and getting massively concerned about the forthcoming encounter. Sometimes making myself physically ill with the stress.

Question:

Have you ever been in serious trouble or reprimanded at work because of an incident that happened due to drink?

Did that make you change the way you behave or are you just hoping it doesn't happen again?

I also remembered having to meet with either a boss or my colleagues and justify my exorbitant expense account. Even when I owned my own company and I did the books at the end of the month I would balk at the huge expenses bill I had run up, and know the money could have been far better spent.

Worst of all was not being able to remember things. So many times I would put on a clean shirt and find a residual mush of paper in the top pocket. At some stage the mush would have been someone's business card with reasons written on it as to why I should give that person a call. Perhaps it was someone who wanted to buy something; perhaps it was someone with a great idea; or someone who wanted to offer me a job. But instead of getting back to the office and actioning whatever was on the card, or getting home and remembering to take the card out to action the next day, I would forget about it, leave it in the pocket, throw the shirt in the washing machine, and dissolve the information. I must have lost hundreds of opportunities that way and that is no exaggeration. I will never ever know what was on those cards. I will never know what conversations preceded me being given those cards either.

Question:

What have you 'probably' lost as a result of being drunk and forgetful?

Sometimes I would go from one meeting to another in the afternoon, always in a wine bar, and even forget with whom and what I had been talking about an hour before in a previous bar. And can you imagine what it feels like to have a meeting with a potential client and your business colleagues, and your client says to you, 'shall we continue where we left off last time Julian?', and you have no idea what they are talking about? – get out of that one!

Question:

How often have you drawn a complete blank when faced with a situation similar to mine?

Now I am happy to have business meetings at any time of the day. I always remember everything, I take notes and never lose them, I have never lost a business card or an opportunity, and I never ever have to suffer that guilt ridden terror of turning up for work not knowing what awaits me because of unremembered actions the day before. I also no longer make drunken promises I won't be able to keep. If I can't do something or don't want to do something I say so, I don't hide behind a bottle of wine thinking I can simply drink the issue away.

Damocles no longer has his Sword hanging over me

The incredible freedom I feel is not to be underestimated. It also gives me a huge sense of wellbeing, just knowing there is nothing I need to hide or that I'm hiding from. There is no longer a Sword of Damocles hanging over my head.

This is something you will relish regardless of what you do for a living.

So do I miss all those lunches and all that glorious wine?

> My friends and colleagues and I still meet to laugh and chat about similar things we used to, but I generally leave before anyone gets drunk and starts to repeat themselves. I find that so boring it makes me realise what I must have sounded like to anyone I was with who wasn't also drunk. **What an arsehole I was**.

It was certainly one of the things I thought I would miss most and that put me off ever quitting before. I really couldn't imagine what I would do with myself if I was to be forever sober and I had to go back to the office instead of larking about all afternoon. **But then I had never tried**. I had of course had many occasions when I couldn't have a glass at lunchtime or had to limit myself to just one or two, but because I was a drinker this just left me frustrated and dying for the end of the working day so I could race to a wine bar. I would sit in some boring meeting discreetly looking at my watch and thinking what I would have to drink once set 'free' instead of concentrating and trying to enjoy what was going on around me. I remember now the tense feeling I had and the dislike of the people who were keeping me tied to my desk for whatever reason rather than letting me escape and go drinking. This even includes when I had my own business and I had to stay sober to meet with my management in the afternoon.

Question:

How often have you looked at your watch or the clock on the wall in frustration, and wished the person talking would shut up so you could go and have a drink?

I still meet with many of the friends and business colleagues I used to associate with, but far less often. This is not for any reason other than we mainly used to meet just to get drunk together. I would never go and drink at lunchtime on my own in the City, many people do, but I hated the thought of that; of being thought of as an alcoholic or a 'billy no mates'. Instead I had a stock of people I could call who would be up for a lunch, so we could get smashed together and share the guilt of being out all afternoon. Now when I see those same faces I drink a lime and soda or a water and only stay for an hour at most. We still laugh and chat about similar things we used to, but I generally leave before anyone gets drunk and starts to repeat themselves. I find that so boring it makes me realise what I must have sounded like to anyone I was with who wasn't also drunk. What an arsehole I was.

Something I didn't realise when I was drinking was

just how unreliable and potentially unpredictable I was. One of my clients is a Paris based company that invites all its staff to a weekend all-expenses-paid skiing adventure in the French Alps every year. I had never been invited and I assumed this was because I wasn't on the payroll, just a consultant. Now I don't drink, all of a sudden I'm a welcome guest and the reason I was never previously made welcome has finally sunk in. I have been twice now and had a fantastic time even though I have been one of the very few of the hundred or so attendees not drinking at all (the other couple of non-drinkers are strict Muslim). Another reason I never minded not having been invited is that I don't or didn't ski. I took both my daughters skiing a few years ago and had a try myself but hated it. The fact I was so stiff with gout and in constant pain might have been a factor in that. Now, although I avoid the slopes I have learnt Nordic skiing, and being fit and gout free I can enjoy all day trekking through the mountains and forests and I love every minute of it. Even the après ski is enjoyable not having to worry about pacing how much alcohol I consume so as not to make a fool of myself.

Question:

Have you thought what you might be missing, or you are not invited to be part of because others see you as unreliable or even worse, as a liability?

Work life regrets

I have to admit I have been very lucky and I have made sufficient money to be comfortable. If I really could turn the clock back would I change much? Well if I had shown an interest at school, found that I had a love of science and gone on to university, I could have been a mining engineer and travelled the world earning vast sums of money and retiring on a huge pension. If I had stayed focused and worked for just one company for a long time I could have made it to an executive position and also travelled the planet earning vast sums. If I had tried teaching much earlier on I could be headmaster of a school by now and be helping a whole generation to succeed in life. There are a lot of ifs I could list but there is no point. The really important thing is that I now look forward with an attitude that says I can **still** achieve great things. I **can** be a famous author and travel the world and earn vast sums of money (if that is what I still wanted, although my philosophy has changed markedly – see chapter later). I **can** still be a successful businessman, start a new company and travel. I **can** try teaching again if I want, or travel overseas and teach. I **can** write a self-help book on drinking and help other people change their lives. In other words whereas I thought my life was ending and even that it would be over by this date, I now look forward to many more decades on this planet where the only limits on what I achieve will be the ones I impose upon myself, or are dictated by the degree of effort I am prepared to put in. So no, I don't have any regrets, but I do make sure I have learnt and continue to learn from my past experiences both good and bad. You can't change what has happened but if you don't learn from it, what was the point of it happening at all.

> You can't change what has happened, but if you don't learn from it, what was the point of it happening at all?

Question:

What aspirations do you have for your career / work-life that are unlikely to happen unless you make changes to your lifestyle?

Just how realistic are those aspirations if you stay as you are and what do you think your own true potential really is?

Thought:

You might already be hugely successful and wealthy but the fact you are reading this book tells me you are unhappy with your lot. How much better could your daily life be if you didn't drink? Are you drinking because you are scared of, or escaping from something?

Money

I see pictures on the news of people standing outside food banks smoking and think to myself, 'how can they waste money on cigarettes to the extent they have to then rely on a charity hand out to feed themselves and their family?' But in a way I was like that. For so much of my life I have been broke, fortunately never to the extent where I have had to take state benefits, but certainly to the point where I have been on the verge of bankruptcy and been technically insolvent. There was even one day I was with my youngest daughter, she was five at the time and I was a single parent, and the bank machine swallowed my card instead of spewing cash out and that was that, I had no more money. Somehow however, even on that fateful day I managed to find enough loose change in draws, pockets of old suits, down the back of the sofa and elsewhere to be able to buy a packet of fags and a bottle of wine.

There are so many times that for the sake of a few extra pounds or a little less monthly expenditure things would have been very different in my life. This isn't a sob story mind you and not everything was bad. It was because I was so broke I joined the Territorial Army as they paid you a small weekly sum and an annual tax free bonus. If I hadn't been broke I would never have joined, and being in the T.A. I had some of the best times of my life, and did things I would never been otherwise able to do. There weren't many other people crossing London Bridge on a Monday morning who had spent the weekend being in a tank battle on Salisbury plain, or hanging out of a Puma helicopter, or riding in a Chinook. But mainly money has been tight and it wasn't until I gave up drinking (I quit smoking 22 years ago) that I realised just how much I was spending on booze.

In 'I Don't Drink' I estimate I save £10.00 per day through not drinking. This takes into account a bottle and a half of wine at £5.00 per bottle and a three litre bottle of cider. In reality I was spending far more than that.

Even when we definitely couldn't afford it my wife and I were still going out to dinner at least twice a week. This wasn't for the love of food but mainly because it meant I could encourage my wife to drink as well so I would feel less guilty, I wouldn't be seen to be drinking by myself at home with my wife watching disapprovingly, and simply because having no hobbies or other interests at the time it was something to do. No matter what kind of restaurant we ended up in we would always have at least two bottles of wine and probably some liquors as well. If I assume we went out one hundred times in a given year, the booze element of all those meals would equate to at least £2,500, and the whole meal element the same again at least.

Now we go out perhaps once a month, not because we don't want to go out or that we can't afford it but purely because we are so busy doing other things, and we enjoy the pleasure of each other's company over a meal at home. And when we do go out, the bill is a fraction of what it used to be.

If I was then to add what I spent at work on booze the numbers would get silly. To give you some idea, every lunch would involve me buying at least two bottles of wine at £20-25.00 per bottle. Over the course of a year assuming there are 200 working days that is an incredible £10,000.00 on booze alone. No wonder there were raised eyebrows when I put through my expenses, and no wonder I used to have to absorb much of that cost myself.

I remember what it was like every month going through the mountain of receipts I had accumulated and trying to put a spreadsheet together that justified the spend. Some of the receipts had the name of the potential client or client I was with written on them. Sometimes that name would keep cropping up and so I couldn't justify claiming it more than once or twice. Sometimes I had stupidly forgotten or been too drunk to write the name down and so had to either make something up or throw the receipt away. On some days I found I had three receipts for 'lunches' at different times of the day where I had obviously gone from wine bar to wine bar, each time running up a

£50.00 bill and only realising the total impact when I came to account for it all at the end of the month. What a nightmare it all was not only from a monetary sense, but from the stress that accompanied this exercise.

Question:

Do you have to submit expense claims, and how much of an issue with your employer is the drinks element?

Now apart from travel expenses, my expense claim to the company I work for is nil or at the most a few pounds for coffees and teas. The improvement in the relationship I have with my client as a consequence is hugely significant.

So to summarise let's look at what I was spending per annum on booze:

Table 2: average annual spend on alcohol (conservative estimate)

Element	Detail	£ Totals
Daily drinking at home bill	365 days x £10.00 per day	3,650.00
Restaurant drinks element	100 meals x £25.00	2,500.00
	Less 100 x £10.00 as this is accounted for above	- 1,000.00
		1,500.00
Business lunches I had to personally pay for	£10,000 x 0.5 as I generally picked up half of the bills	5,000.00
Total		£ 10,150.00

You might not care what you spend on booze at this

stage. You might be so well off the amount is immaterial but it sometimes pays to put things into perspective especially if you know of items or people on which the money could be far better spent.

I have already spent much of what I have saved so far on luxuries just to treat myself. These include a sports car, holidays to China and India and other non-essential items I would otherwise have had to do without or would have had to go into debt to afford. But I am lucky and have reached that time of life where I have most of what I need. Had I been giving up drinking twenty years earlier the extra money would have gone on clothes and essentials for my children and even a family holiday or two.

But as mentioned earlier, I have been able to reduce the amount of time I spend working by taking less of a wage and this is the **real benefit**. The luxuries are purely that, the extra time I now have and the consequent improved quality of life for those I love are the real things I treasure – the time really is priceless. Once again, if I had quit drinking twenty years ago and swapped the extra money for extra time with my children, how much better things might have been, but that is looking back negatively and I said I wouldn't do that.

> I would swap everything I own for an extra day of life with my wife and family

Question:

How much do you spend on drink? Is this money you can afford to waste or do you consider it good value for money? Have you been broke and wish you had more money? What would you do with a few thousand pounds windfall?

When did you last go to the pub and resent buying a round of drinks because it was a shock how large the bill was? Wouldn't it be better to be drinking something soft and to stay out of the round altogether?

If you had to list how much you spent in a year on one side of a sheet of paper and on the other side list what you could spend that on without feeling guilty or extravagant, what would that look like? Why not give it a go? Have a look at my wish list and note I have **only** taken into account the amount I was spending on booze at home. I have ignored the meals out and the work element.

Annual spend on drink	Wish list
	New refracting telescope £1,500
	Night vision binoculars £500
	Motor scooter £ 1,700
	New Kayak and accessories £ 500
£ 3,650	£ 4,200

If these items seem a bit unnecessary and extravagant we are planning moving home in the next two years and these are things I would like to have to enjoy in the next place we live. And yes I would have to wait an extra couple of months to be able to afford everything.

(I have also kept this list well away from my wife or it would just be scribbled out and the one word 'handbag' would be emblazoned across it!)

Challenge:

What I haven't said is list the things you and your family really need and that by you not drinking, you could pay for. Give that a go if you dare, I never did because I couldn't bear to think how much my drinking was really costing those around me.

*Incidentally my wife did peer over my shoulder so she did see my list. Quite rightly she pointed out that my book is not just for men and that I should include a female version of the list in the book as well. She decided that having seen mine, I could base this on her own wish list which duly follows. Although she doesn't drink so in effect she is not saving anything extra, she explained that the fact she wasn't spending the money in the first place is ample justification for having the same amount of money as me to spend now. She tells me this is sound logic.

Annual spend on drink	Wish list
	Mulberry handbag £ 1,000
	Matching Mulberry accessories £ 500
	New wardrobe and shoes £ 3,500
	Perfumes and sundry items £ 500
	Camera and accessories £ 900
£ 0	£ 6,400

Obviously her list far exceeds her budget if she is to have the same amount to spend as me, but she very sensibly suggested she could borrow from my fund. She caveated this by rightly pointing out that with so much light pollution around these days I could always manage without the telescope, the scooter would be too dangerous for me to ride and she would never dare ride pillion, and that I probably wouldn't use the night vision binoculars much anyway as I tend to go to bed quite early. At least that still leaves me a new kayak to look forward to, but then that was for her anyway!

Health

Former drinker halts 'dangerous' disease

I state at the beginning of this book that I want to keep things positive and not harp on about all the negative reasons why you should quit alcohol. But what I will do is restress what has changed for me since I quit because if you decide to do the same, your health will also dramatically improve.

In my book 'I Don't Drink!' I list the obvious changes to my life that were apparent at 250 days of no alcohol. Many of these became realised far earlier than this, but 250 days was a good milestone and I was so over the moon with the new me I decided to produce a list of benefits to send to my daughters. I reproduce the health aspects of that list here, with some relevant notes since added as the original list was produced two years ago:

- My blood pressure has reduced way down to 116/70 and I have been told to come off the tablets I had been on for ten years. (It has now settled at a regular 130/68 without medication, more than acceptable for someone of my age and with my background.)

- My heart rate averages at 52 – this is athlete status. (I have since been seen by a specialist as this rate is deemed to be low, but having been tested on the treadmill they now appreciate it is only low because I am exceptionally fit for my age.)

- My high cholesterol has gone and I have been taken off the tablets. (Two years on it remains at the normal level and therefore any issue of high cholesterol has gone altogether.)

- **My type 2 diabetes has gone away.** (I didn't realise how serious a disease this was at the time, and I played down the fact my type 2 had gone away. I was still being regularly monitored however, and it was not until July 2015 that a diabetes specialist was finally content to say the disease had been resolved and I was taken off the watch list and off their database.) They put my beating the disease firmly down to lifestyle change which included losing the excess weight, stopping drinking and changing my diet to cut out sausages, burgers and the other unhealthy muck I was eating.

- My gout has gone (and NEVER come back!)
- I have lost nearly two stone in weight and I am now a 32/33 inch waist down from 36 – my weight has now settled at 13 stones (182 pounds) despite all the extra muscle I have put on.) (**See the separate section on weight loss**.)
- My psoriasis has vanished. (This was something I had from childhood and it was especially bad on my elbows and knees with occasional patches on my hands and face. It has never come back and I suspect constant dehydration from the alcohol was stopping it being resolved.)
- My fingernails have cleared up and look normal. (I caught an infection in 1999 which never went away.)
- All my body functions work as they should! (I will say no more than that I am as normal as I imagine I should be – it wasn't always so when I was drinking!)
- My breath is fresher, I only ever have a nice taste in my mouth and my taste-buds work much better than they ever did. (I also have

noticeably brighter eyes, softer hair and healthier looking skin.)

Question:

What would you like to improve about your health? And on the basis of my list, are there things in your list you recognise might improve or be cured if you quit alcohol?

Of the hidden benefits you can't immediately see for yourself without the benefit of an x-ray, a scan or a blood test, I knew by 250 days that my liver would be regenerating (I now have a new one if medical science is to be believed), my kidneys would have had a good clear out and my brain would be losing far less cells than it used to.

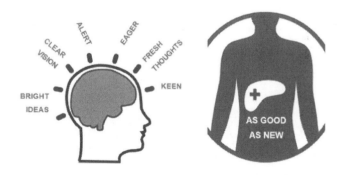

The kidney issue led to a question in my own mind recently:

Assuming it was compatible, would I be able to donate a kidney to my wife or one of my children/grandson if they needed it? Would I have been able to do so when the kidneys were pickled with booze? The answer is I don't know, but I am sure I would have a far better chance of being to help them now than I would have done three years ago. And on a more morbid note, I am sure most of my body parts have a far better chance of being of some use to someone else after I have vacated this body than they would have been. It's nice to think my body is worthy of a little more than simply being chucked in the bin because **I was the one who trashed it.**

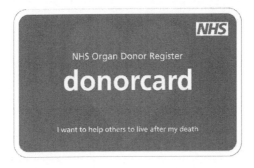

Thought:

I know I would have felt devastated if I had been asked to donate one of my kidneys to help my wife or one of my daughters, but the surgeons had then turned me down because my kidneys were wrecked through years of alcohol abuse.

But to conclude this section on a really positive note and to top the list above, I now feel so much younger and I have so much more stamina, energy, zest, zip, spark of life and whatever else you want to call it. I also expect to live somewhat longer than I had planned before! So most important of all by a mile:

> **I swapped a 5 year life expectancy for a 45 year life expectancy!**

Question:

How long do you expect to live? Until your 60's, 70's 80's or longer? And what do you think your quality of life will be like if you simply carry on as you are? Will you end up in a home, sitting in front of a TV and vegetating because you are too unfit and unhealthy to do otherwise?

I knew with confidence I wouldn't end up in a home or something similar, because not expecting to live that long the possibility didn't enter my head. It still amazes me that I thought I would be dead by now – when I think of all the things I am now doing and experiencing that I would have missed out on!

Question:

How do you think your expected lifespan and your quality of life might change if you quit drinking?

The first part of that question is a difficult one to ask and the answer depends on so much - as the saying goes 'who knows what life will bring.' But one thing is for sure – no matter what state you are in at the moment, if you quit alcohol and by so doing get fitter, healthier, wake up your brain and create a new positive you, every year from now on will be an improvement and you will be the one to thank for that. It will be **you** who made the effort.

Weight loss

I have never dieted as such and as mentioned earlier I have always tried to stay fairly fit. (I did have a beer gut in my twenties and like most men in that condition, I was inordinately proud of it!) It was a bit of a surprise therefore when the doctor diagnosed me with Type 2 diabetes and told me one of the things I needed to do was lose weight. It's only when you see pictures of yourself you realise just how much weight you are carrying. Here is one of me in Sicily looking suitably horrific (at the time I thought how cool I looked!)

My diet at the time was based around lots of sausages and lots of cheese, washed down with all the wine and cider. Not the best of diet you might say and after the doctor's kind words I did make an effort by cutting down on some of the cheese but nothing else. I thought if I increased my exercise routine that would lose the weight for me but unfortunately the gout didn't allow for this.

Before I quit alcohol I was probably addicted to sausages. I would barbecue almost every night and eat six or seven sausages with baked potatoes and baked beans or salad. I would also add about a quarter pound of cheese on top and swill the whole lot down with the booze.

To quit alcohol I had to give up the barbecuing as I thought it would be too hard being outside in all weathers cooking away and not being able to have a drink, and I didn't want to chance it. I decided therefore to join my wife in being a pescetarian – someone who only eats fish and vegetables (she wouldn't have allowed me to wreck the oven by cooking my sausages indoors anyway.) Luckily her cooking is fantastic, and so despite my previous view that vegetarian food was rabbit fodder, the menu she serves up is delicious.

Once I had quit the alcohol I found I started craving sweet foods such as cakes and puddings, things I had never eaten before. Obviously my body was trying to make up for all the sugar it wasn't getting in the booze. I had never considered alcohol to be fattening and full of calories, I don't think people really do. Buy I now know I was drinking the equivalent of eight burgers every day, and that on top of my actual food!

But despite this the weight fell away. I know I was able to increase my exercise routine as the gout had gone, but even being on a pescetarian diet I was eating a huge amount of food. The one thing I did avoid was replacing alcohol with fizzy drinks like Coke. I stuck to water and squashes instead. I have a friend who also quit alcohol and has managed nearly ten years alcohol free, but he became addicted to cola and was drinking ten to twelve pints of the stuff per day. He ended up looking like Father Christmas.

So if weight loss is one of the reasons you want to consider quitting alcohol, it does work, but from the letters and feedback I receive it can take time and a lot depends on your individual make-up. I now manage the amount of cakes and puddings I eat but I do have at least some biscuits every day, and I always finish my evening meal with a large bowl of fruit crumble and ice cream! – washed down with a few pints of clean fresh water of course.

Why did it take me so long to wake up to the health benefits from quitting alcohol?

In reading the above chapter on health you might well wonder why it took me so long to wake up to reality and to quit alcohol.

Perhaps it's the way the effects of alcohol creep up on you. The obvious and more immediate impacts such as a hangover are simple to pin down, other effects such as gout are easy to excuse as being something other than drink related, and even high blood pressure and high cholesterol can be blamed on diet or inherited genes. The hidden impacts of course such as liver disease, kidney malfunction and cancer don't become apparent until it's almost too late.

In any event, if you have any health issues for which you know the cause is probably drink related, **and because you don't want to stop drinking**, you will tend to ignore them or simply learn to live with them. I was a great one for denying any of my ailments were drink related.

But I also blame the media and the health organisations that are supposed to encourage abstinence. Let's look at some examples:

1   The daily safe allowance that governments recommend just provides a comfort blanket to hide under. In the UK, for men they recommend no more than 3-4 units per day and 2-3 units for women.

I always read this as 4 units not 3-4. I also assumed there were two fudge factors in this figure. Firstly, being a six foot male of substantial build I was above average and so I could go to 5 units without feeling guilty. Secondly, just like the speed limit on the roads, no-one is expected to stick to this religiously and everyone (quite wrongly) knows you can exceed the speed limit by ten miles per hour without the Police stopping you. Equating this to alcohol, if 30 mph equals 40 mph, then 5 units equals 7 units. Without trying I have almost doubled my daily limit!

Question:

Have you tried a similar mind game with alcohol limits, or speed limits for that matter?

2   We have all read stories in the press about how most doctors are either alcoholics or at least have a drink problem. Whether this is true or not it provides a great excuse not to take their advice. I also observe that many medical profession workers these days are obese, so once again this hardly allows them room to moralise against others for their shortcomings.

3   Many alcohol related reports I see tend to point out the harm alcohol does to you but at the same time emphasise just how big a problem this is nationwide or even worldwide. Being told that fifty-five per cent of men my age drink more than the recommended guidelines just gave me yet another excuse to hide behind.

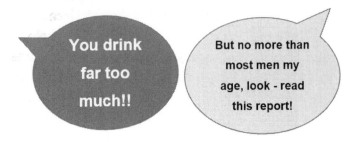

'You drink far too much!' my wife would sometimes shout.

'I drink about the same as half the population!' I would shout back.

Question:

Have you ever used a 'not just me' excuse to justify to yourself that you don't have a drink issue?

There isn't an answer to this of course, especially as there is considerable vested interest at play. A cynic might say that if no-one drank to excess there wouldn't be a need for all the countless companies making a fortune offering rehab and counselling sessions (or the need for authors of books like this, although not making fortunes I hasten to add.)

What I would like to see are more examples cited of people like me who have changed their lives and turned their back on alcohol. Not people 'living with alcoholism' and how they are being helped by such and such an organisation, but real cases of people who no longer need anyone else's help. I suppose that sort of story doesn't attract the same degree of readership, or the same level of charity donations or public funding. But then I AM a cynic.

Fitness

Question:

What sporting activities do you do and how happy are you with your performance? Do you think or know you could improve your performance if you didn't drink?

Perhaps you don't do any sport at all. Perhaps you don't get much exercise either and perhaps the reason for that is you drink too much.

It is almost unnecessary to talk about what doing sports and other exercise is like once you have quit drinking because you already know it is going to be easier, better and more fun.

Swimming was the one exercise I did regularly before I quit. I would tell myself I swam three to four times a week which is what I used to do in my thirties, but in reality I only swam twice a week. Even so I would manage a kilometre (40 lengths of a 25 metre pool) in just over twenty minutes, a fast time for breaststroke. Even if I had gout I would swim but I would have to use a float and swim just using my arms.

Another sport I tried was horse-riding and I was very good at this, but on one occasion I had to have my right boot cut off because my foot had swollen up so much during the ride and I never went again.

Walking was something I also used to enjoy but often I would suffer afterwards with swollen knees which might cripple me for days. In fact my legs were so bad at times, I couldn't kneel down, I couldn't walk anywhere bare foot, and I certainly wouldn't have been able to run.

Naturally, I put everything down to age!

What sporting activities do I do now?

I still swim but now I really do swim at least five times per week, sometimes every day. My lap times are about the same but often I swim for a mile (1.6 kilometres) and I do a lot more mixed stroke swimming including backstroke and crawl. Sometimes I swim in the local pool and then also have a swim in the sea after kayaking.

Kayaking

I am lucky in that I live by the sea so between March and October I kayak whenever the weather permits and I have the time. I average about ten kayak outings per month.

I do generally wear a wet suit but I kayak for an hour or so and then have a swim in the sea to finish off. If the water is clear I will also snorkel under the lifeboat station at Selsey where there is always lots of interesting marine life to explore.

I did have the kayak before I quit drinking but I only used it once or twice, even getting it up the shingle beach from the water was too painful for my feet and knees. As I say, I just felt too old. Now I have two friends I kayak with, one is twenty-eight so he makes me feel young in that I am as fit as he is, and the other one is seventy-eight, and he makes me feel really young because I now know I am!

Karate

One of my dreams was to be a karate black belt and you will now know I never did anything about taking up the sport.

I deliberately started having lessons a few months after having quit alcohol just so I could actually achieve something I had always promised to myself.

What has surprised me is how easily I am able to

cope with the circuit training that is a necessary part of the lesson's warm-up, and which involves a lot of running and hopping around the gym barefoot, and doing press-ups and sit-ups. To think I couldn't even walk barefoot before I quit drinking is simply amazing.

I now go once a week for an hour and I practice at home. I thoroughly enjoy it and I am steadily progressing through the ranks, working towards my green belt as I write this. I am probably at least five years away from becoming a black belt – but I will get there.

Scuba diving

I don't go often because it isn't cheap if you don't have your own equipment, but I make sure I do scuba dive at least twice a year here in the UK and more times overseas if it is available where we go on holiday.

You should be fit to scuba dive safely and I have dived with a lot of fit, elderly people in the past so it is something I should be able to carry on doing forever. Ten years ago I thought my diving days were over.

If you ever want to experience alien life try scuba diving – and you get to feel like a hero!

Walking

I always thought walking was boring and used to hate those 'idiots' who march along with the walking poles. Now my wife and I walk for at least an hour every day if not more. Not only am I fit enough to walk on top of all the other exercise I do, I have the time. Sometimes on the weekend we will go for a 10-15 mile hike just for the joy of it and yes – I even have a set of walking poles! (I am the ultimate hypocrite as well as being a cynic.)

So no longer am I sat in front of the TV in the evening with a bottle of wine wasting my life away. If I am not busy writing we walk to enjoy the fresh air, experience the outdoors and the night skies and to give our minds time to think and plan. Even the thought of driving to the local shops is now anathema to me, when I can walk instead.

As an author, walking is a wonderful time to plot my next chapter, think through a strategy or develop a new character.

Others

I could add dancing, cycling, my once a year skiing and the fact we are going to go back to horse-riding into this mix, but hopefully the message is clear.

These are all things I either couldn't do, couldn't contemplate doing, or couldn't do as often or so well when I was a drinker, now the sky's the limit and on that note I might even try a parachute jump to celebrate my 60th! – I just need to find a book 'How to cure a fear of heights!'

Question:

What fitness activities do you do now and how well would you rate your performance?

What activities could you see yourself taking up if you were fitter and you felt younger?

It's a good time for another story, and I have inserted this one here because it involves swimming – sort of...

A story – In the Drink!

I now shun the very idea of drinking anything other than nice refreshing water after an intensive swim, it was not always the case.

As alluded to earlier, my inauguration into working in the London insurance market was just as much one of how well I could hold my drink as of how well I could perform my job. Every lunchtime would involve drinking two to three pints of real ale at an ancient tavern on Fenchurch Street with perhaps a sandwich thrown in for good measure to provide some stomach lining, and then moving on to one of the wonderful City wine bars to drink as much as possible before they closed in those days at 3.00 p.m. My favourite of these haunts included the Grapeshots in Artillery Lane just off Frying Pan Alley, the whole area dating back to pre-Dickensian times and reeking of history; The George and Vulture mentioned many times in Dickens' drunken comedy Pickwick Papers and where Charles is supposed to have written most of that novel; The Jamaica Wine House next door and a favourite with the 17th Century diarist and probable alcoholic Samuel Pepys; and nearer to the office where I was based, the City Flogger in a basement off Fen court with its steep steps you could easily fall up and hurt yourself on your way out. (I know this because I entertained an insurance underwriter there who after three bottles of wine to drink fell and broke his jaw on the way out. Nothing was seen of him for six weeks after which he returned to work all patched up but with a permanent eye twitch which made him wink constantly. After a few days he disappeared again for another few weeks. It turned out he had been unwillingly winking at some yob on the train who thought my underwriter friend had been trying to seduce him, had taken offence, and once again broken his jaw for him.)

Little thought was given to working in the afternoon as everyone in the office from senior management down would be similarly inebriated, the only difference being the calibre of the establishment you had been frequenting and the quality of the wine you had been imbibing which of course improved markedly as you rose through the company's ranks. The really top management even went to restaurants where you sat down and ate food!

This way of operating had carried on happily for three hundred years ever since ship owners started transacting insurance business in Edward Lloyd's coffee shop and until, just like in both World Wars and three years into my insurance career, the Americans came late onto the scene, bought up most of the insurance broking houses and tried to introduce their own work ethic. They simply wouldn't listen to the argument that all this drinking and socialising was where the business was actually being done. (*By the way, Lloyds of London had already been providing insurance for a hundred years when the American Declaration of Independence was signed, so who were they to tell us what to do.*)

In the company where I worked, one of the strict new rules for lowly staff was that unless you could prove to be with an actual client and you were seen to be drinking at lunchtime you could be dismissed. A cunning plan needed to be devised.

Now this new regime coincided with my elder brother Paul and I who both happened to work in the same building but for different divisions of the same broker, also having joined the Territorial Army, and as part of our keep fit programme we would go for a swim at 12.00 every lunchtime to the wonderful Victorian era Whitechapel Baths. Nothing much had changed in this establishment for decades to the point where the boiler would often break down and anyone who dared would be offered a free swim in the freezing water. They also had the old fashioned cages to put your clothes and valuables in and throughout the always cold corridors sound echoed due to the high ceilings and ceramic tiled walls. Paul and I would swim half a mile at a fairly swift pace, often to be overtaken by a mystery stunning blonde in an emerald one-piece bathing costume who like some storybook mermaid would appear in the water as if from nowhere, power past us swimming perfect butterfly and then disappear before we had finished. We never did find out who this vision was.

We would exit the Baths feeling fantastically fit, virtuous and with a warm glow both inside and out, imagining ourselves to be surrounded by a golden energy field like the children in a breakfast cereal advert on TV. Mid-winter was best of all when you could feel your skin tingle as you walked into the cold air and could stride along in just a suit jacket when everyone else was wrapped in coats, scarfs and hats. We also enjoyed as I still do, moistening and rubbing the backs of our hands after our swim and smelling the faint evocative scent of chlorine. *(We now know that wonderful smell is in fact from chloramines produced as a result of chlorine mixing with urine and sweat, but who cares, it smells great.)* But after our exercise and it being now one o'clock and still lunchtime we would be desperate for refreshment, and so to quench our thirsts Paul and I would make our way purposefully to Aunty May's teashop and where upon our arrival we would loudly announce:

'Two teas please May'.

Aunty May's teashop (á la the Five Lamps Wine Bar) was so termed by Paul and I for two reasons. Firstly the old woman who worked behind the bar and whose real name we never bothered to find out because she happily answered to May, looked the image of the May who used to babysit for us and who was labelled Aunty May by our parents, possibly to make her seem kind, caring and trustworthy. And secondly, being aware of the horrid new restrictions upon us, she would serve us up ice cold Luncheon Dry sherry in white china tea cups, and from a special wine bottle capacity teapot she kept by just for us two boys. Imagine the satisfaction of standing at the counter being observed and scrutinised by miserable faced fellow employees, themselves having to subsist on fruit juice, whilst we acted as if we were simply drinking black tea but were in fact enjoying the wonderful sensation of ice cold liquid sherry coursing its way down and around our hot and parched insides, and feeling that nice mellow calming effect as the alcohol rapidly got to work on our dehydrated selves. Most lunchtimes we could manage a pot of tea each before the effects became too apparent and we moved on to tumblers of white wine cleverly disguised by being served from a lemonade jug.

The original May first started babysitting for us when we lived at West Wickham in the county of Kent in the south of England. That was a town renowned in my young life for having a dentist who didn't believe in using gas or injections to deaden the pain; a large jolly doctor who was a no nonsense sort of fellow who rather than send you to a specialist or to hospital, believed in sorting things out for himself which if that involved stabbing you with a sharp knife or cutting suspect bits off you he would do it there and then, using his huge bulk to good effect by sitting on you to restrain you whilst he hacked away (he had also been to the same grin and bear it school of pain control as the dentist); and a scary local woodland with a supposedly haunted lightning tree mentioned in the Domesday book, itself a name to conjure nightmares into an infant head. It was also where Aunty May first introduced us to witchcraft and made terrifying goblins and other 'fairy' creatures run around my room and bounce on the bed at night.

It was Aunty May who first gave Paul and I the camouflaged teapot idea although it took some twenty years for us to realise our own version. From when we first new her she would insist on only drinking anything from her own 'special' teapot which she always brought with her. Although we never tasted the contents, we knew it to be a brown liquid which smelt strong and made your eyes water if you tried to peer down the spout, and when empty she would top it up from a dark glass bottle kept in her copious bag. She also kept jars of pickled onions and beetroot in that bag and would sit watching TV with us, munching from the jars, sipping her special tea and then farting loudly, always blaming the noise on there probably being someone at the back door in which direction she would look.

Her shouts of 'back door' would become more regular as the evening progressed as would her consumption of tea, and often we would wake in the morning to hear mother complain of having returned home to find Aunty May passed out and beetroot having been thrown at the walls. All was forgiven however, because being a witch she would tell the parents' fortunes and they believed every silly word she said.

When we were a few years older and my younger brother Timothy was also on the scene, we moved some distance away to Beckenham, and despite the inconvenience of having to go and fetch her Aunty May remained the main family babysitter, although another 'pseudo aunty' called Molly was sometimes brought in instead. I don't think Aunty Molly drank but she was very hairy, smelt bad, also farted a lot and would sometimes bring along her bearded little mother for company. These two had no idea how to control children and little interest in anything but watching TV or calling up spirits from the afterlife, so we would most often disappear for the evening getting up to all sorts of really bad mischief. But as Molly was a psychic and also told fortunes the parents once again forgave all faults. In fact Molly became the main babysitter after Aunty May refused to come any more, I remember May's final evening spent with us.

Aunty May was in a bad mood because despite being forbidden to leave the house as he had been suspected (rightly it turned out) of setting fire to a local cricket pavilion the previous evening, Paul (who May always referred to as a sod and a half) had laughed at her and gone out anyway. It was also a hot evening, I was insistent upon listening to 'Top of the Pops' really loud on the TV and Timmy refused go to bed. I remember her getting crosser and crosser and drinking heavily from the teapot, and then when it was empty hugging and rubbing it like it had some genie inside. As the evening wore on and Paul still hadn't returned she started stamping round the house, shouting at Timmy and I, and she then shut herself in the lounge where we could hear her tinkling around in Dad's drinks cabinet, mumbling to herself, and occasionally screaming obscenities. As all this did was to make Timmy and I laugh we thought we would make things even funnier by quickly opening the lounge door, and letting Paul's pet budgie Sammy loose inside. Not only did Aunty May hate birds, she especially detested Sammy because he had been taught to sing 'Aunty May's a bastard' which of course he did over and over again as we wet ourselves giggling outside the door. This was too much for May. She threw open the door and stamped towards us threatening to kill us just as Paul came through the front door with two teenage friends. As May turned on them instead, Paul simply picked her up (he was bigger than her by now), and carried the struggling and screaming babysitter around the hallway, into the kitchen and then locked her in the pantry.

After that I seem to recall my parents gave up and simply left us to our own devices, Aunty Molly only being paid to turn up in case any neighbours came round and found us boys 'home alone'. I am amazed that despite their ardent soothsaying powers neither May or Molly ever foresaw what we boys were going to getup to!

Entertainment

> How would I cope every day for the rest of my life desperately wanting a drink and not being able to have one?

I don't watch much TV I have to admit, but I used to. I think I just grew out of TV when I was living at the cottage because there was so much atmosphere being in the countryside, I didn't want to just sit indoors and stare at a screen for hours. Besides, just like most other things in my life I had 'been there and done that'.

I used to watch soaps on TV and sometimes even watch the whole week's episodes again when the BBC ran their weekend omnibus edition. I used to watch sport, especially rugby and formula one motor racing. I watched sitcoms and movies and the news and just about anything else that was on. I would especially watch late evening rubbish but purely because there was nothing else on and it was an excuse not to go to bed so I could have another drink. I even got to know many of the adverts so well I could relay every second of them and even now I could probably write a book about my favourite adverts I have seen since I was a child. In the days when TV wasn't broadcasting all day I had even been caught sitting and watching the testcard for hours!

But perhaps my favourite time was Sunday afternoon after a lovely lunch and sitting down with a bottle of red wine to watch a movie on TV.

How could I possibly give all that enjoyment up and not miss it? Can you imagine life without your favourite TV programmes and enjoying watching them with a glass of something alcoholic in your hand?

Well of course the answer is you don't have to give up watching anything when you quit drinking, you just might want to avoid some particular programmes for a short while.

Not so *Ab Fab*

One of my favourite sitcoms was/is *absolutely fabulous.* I have always liked films and programmes with Joanna Lumley in them but then I met her when I was a teenager, danced with her and even kissed her so I would wouldn't I? I loved all the boozing in *ab fab*, the maniac lifestyle, the kitchen with the fridge bursting with Bollinger champagne and Stolichnaya vodka (something I wanted in my house) and the total champagne lifestyle, something I dreamt of leading.

I dreaded watching *ab fab* once I had quit drinking, I

was sure just seeing the two women boozing and having so much fun would surely make me want a drink. It was two years after I quit I finally got round to watching the very first episode from the first series on DVD.

I hated it at first. I didn't realise how averse to alcohol I had become in the interim. Perhaps because I have naturally avoided being around drunks since I gave up, it was a bit of a shock seeing two people completely wrecked and my being supposed to find it wildly amusing. I also found it stupid and unrealistic. Watching the two of them cavort around from shop to bar to shop to bar and all the time drinking, I remembered having done very much the same and how at some stage I ran out of steam. Not only that but I came over ill, needed to have a lie down and the following day swore never to drink that much again. That sort of lifestyle is a recipe for wrecked health, wrecked relationships and a wrecked life. The last thing watching this episode did was make me want a drink, in fact it had the complete opposite effect.

Because my wife also loves *ab fab* we persevered and I enjoyed episode two and the subsequent episodes as much as I had ever done. It was like watching them with a child's eyes never having had an alcoholic drink. I realised then and there that I could watch anything with drinking in it by seeing it in a similar way, after all I used to enjoy films where drinking was going on long before I ever tasted alcohol so apart from now knowing what they were doing, what was so different?

Question:

What programmes / films do you think you might have a problem watching if you didn't drink anymore, and why? Here are some more of mine.

James Bond **films.** All that martini shaken and not stirred, yet more Bollinger, the best of wines and all in such cool settings. Would Mr. Bond look so cool having a green tea? Perhaps not, but him ordering a glass of iced mountain water might sound cool, and the fact he would be 100% sober might have more of an impact on his adversaries than him being pissed and slow to react.

The Darling Buds of May. A superb UK TV comedy drama series based around a family in the 1950's and starring that wonderful comedy actor David Jason. Watching this always gave me the excuse to drink whenever in the day I felt like it, just as the family seem to do in the programme. I love the line 'milk or Johnny Walker?' when Pam Ferris offers morning tea to her future son-in-law. I now know I would have just as much summer fun as they do but sticking instead to ginger beer or cloudy lemonade.

Ice Cold in Alex. The classic wartime drama with John Mills and Sylvia Syms. After spending the whole film building up an enormous thirst playing in the desert with an old ambulance, the cast end up in a bar in Alexandria and drool as the barman pours each of them an ice cold frothy pint of lager. A mouth-watering scene. I must have first watched this film when I was about eight years old and I had never tasted beer then so didn't understand what they were drinking, other than it looked refreshing. It probably sent me running to mother to pour me a glass of squash or fizzy lemonade.

If I had never been an alcoholic, I know watching that film now would probably send me scurrying into the kitchen for a cold beer, but I have been an alcoholic and now I don't drink so there is no point even thinking about having one. I have switched my mind off to even considering going down that avenue of drinking again, and so it really truly doesn't bother me at all.

> **I genuinely thought I would have to hide away from anything promoting drink.**

And as for all those adverts, if I see an advert for drink I sometimes feel like shouting out to the smiley-silly people on the film about to swallow the booze, 'Don't do it!' I really do get quite affronted by them. For me, it's a bit like it would be going to the cinema and before the film comes on, being shown adverts for heroin or hugely obese people eating plates of burgers, it really turns me off. Not that I have become a prude, it's just not the reaction I thought I would have to all this potential stimulation - I genuinely thought I would have to hide away from anything promoting drink.

Question:

Do alcohol adverts stimulate you to want a drink?

Do you think they still would if you had given up?

A night at the opera?

I don't really like opera so the title should read ballet or play or concert, but let's face it, one of the fun things about the theatre is going to the nice cosy bar before it starts and getting just that little bit merry. It's especially nice if you have also pre-ordered your interval drinks and they are there all lined up waiting for you at half time.

If we go out now I skip going to the bar before the show starts unless my wife wants anything, and for the interval I pre-order a nice pot of green tea for myself and I encourage my wife to have one of those small bottles of champagne (you see, I am still a nightmare when it comes to bullying others to drink). I have to say I am so cured from wanting anything alcoholic I don't miss the drinking experience part of going out at all, but I do look forward to having one of those nice tubs of ice cream. There are a few other things I don't miss either:-

- Not being able to drive home from the theatre because I am over the limit.
- Queuing for a drink and worrying that I won't have time to enjoy it before the bell goes and the show starts.
- Worrying that someone else has nicked my pre-ordered drinks or that the wine will be warm or there is no ice in the gin and tonic.
- Drinking my glass of wine (if that is all I ordered) so fast in the interval I need to queue for another one which means I might not have time to drink it and that I am ignoring the people I am with.
- If in my greed I have ordered a whole bottle of wine, panicking that I won't be able to drink the whole bottle in the ten minutes of so they give you or that people will start noticing and I will come across as a complete drunken sot.
- Getting pissed and spilling the wine in my haste.
- Falling asleep in the second half of the show – almost an inevitability.
- Missing whatever it was I was supposed to be awake to see / hear.
- Being nagged for getting pissed and ruining

what should have been a nice evening.
- The expensive bar bill.
- Feeling rotten the next day.

Question:

How many of the above do you recognise in yourself?

Sports events

I never really went to many sports events but if I did they were normally through work and hospitality based. The sort of things I was lucky enough to be invited to included cricket, rugby and tennis, all things you could happily watch whilst knocking back a glass or bottle of something.

Since giving up alcohol and because my work style has changed I have only been invited to one event and that was a day at Wimbledon. I had always wanted to go to Wimbledon ever since I was a child but had never had (or made) the opportunity to attend. In later years I imagined how grand an affair it would be with champagne and strawberries and being able to watch the tennis in a half drunken but pleasant fug.

Visiting Wimbledon as a non-drinker was probably a bit unique as there seemed to be drink on offer everywhere albeit it at vastly inflated prices, but I stuck with tea and lime and soda and had just as much fun as the crowd I was with. It was also nice to arrive home feeling fresh and lively, full of interesting stories and still with some life in me as opposed to being hungover, tired and too exhausted to talk.

Question:

Do you go to major sporting events with friends, and would you find it a challenge not to drink at them? You might have to give them a miss or offer to drive and be the hero.

And so to bed...

It goes without saying that the more intimate side to your life is likely to improve. I will leave it at that.

The following short story goes to show how much fun (mostly I am ashamed to say at other peoples' expense) my family had being drunks. The events depicted are not atypical, so at least I can truly look back and say I have been there and done that...

A story – Watch with mother!

'He looks like Tarzan!' my mother shouted.

She had to yell to be heard over the full orchestra at the London Coliseum busy playing Berlioz's introduction to the famous ballet *Le Spectre de la Rose*. Tarzan of course was none other than the world's most famed ballet dancer Rudolf Nureyev dancing the part of the rose, and he had just swung into view from the right of the stage holding tightly to a creeper. Mother and father were sitting at the other end of the stalls from my wife and I and I could see her also waving to attract my attention, but despite our close proximity to the dancers I couldn't see if Rudolf, like me, was grinning at my mother's remark. Certainly the sighs of indignation from the other two thousand plus people in the audience indicated that they were less than impressed, but so what, Mum never cared what others thought as far as our own entertainment was concerned, especially after she had spoken to a pint or two of Dom Perignon. Incidentally, the ballet that evening was being performed by the appropriately named 'Nancy Ballet Company', and world renowned Prima Ballerina Margo Fontaine was already on stage pretending to be asleep and dreaming, and probably not expecting to be awoken from her slumber with the announcement,

'Oooh, he nearly hit Jane!'

Another fairly regular performance which was perhaps just as 'Nancy' occurred every time we went with Mum to her favourite restaurant across the road from her apartment in Brighton. The Regency restaurant in Regency Square is famous for its fish and is ideally situated opposite what was once West Pier (where they filmed the wonderful World War One satire *Oh! What a Lovely War*). Unfortunately all that's now left of the pier is a wreckage of iron work following years of neglect, storms, a highly suspicious fire although nothing to do with either my brother or myself, and the singular inability of the West Pier Trust to decide what to do with it, which ended up with them losing agreed Lottery funding for a restoration project. Fortunately despite years of having to cope with regular visits from my family the Regency Restaurant is not in ruins and is still going strong. Even the most well-behaved of evenings spent there would end up with us all wearing silly hats and bonnets, singing at the tops of our voices, generally annoying our fellow diners by being far too loud and invasive and trying to get them to join in especially if they were foreigners, and being the last to leave after many many bottles of wine and glasses of tongue blackening Strega. My brother Paul looked especially fearsome in a chef's hat and holding a cleaver, pretending to have stormed from the kitchen and picking on anyone who had dared to leave anything uneaten on their plate. But what especially used to upset and disturb diners on nearby tables once the lights had been dimmed and the candles brought out were our late evening séances. The group on our table would steer our loud conversation round to mysticism and the occult, and pretend we were going to summon someone from the 'other side'. We would talk about the afterlife and suchlike and look upwards as if someone was watching over us, all thus guaranteeing interest from anyone sitting within earshot. Then once we had hooked our audience (quite appropriate for a fish restaurant) we would hold hands around our table, all would go deathly quiet, I would start breathing deeply and heavily and then pretend to go into a trance. All the other diners would stare at us transfixed and in nervous anticipation as we focused our eyes down at the table top and sat motionless for what would have seemed ages. Then, as I slowly raised my head whilst looking upwards to try and show just the whites of my eyes, in a deep baritone voice I would say the immortal words:

'Is there anybody there?'

And at that cue, Paul and I would lift the table with our knees and make it seem to zoom around as we and everyone else in the restaurant screamed.

The Melrose restaurant next door to the Regency had it even worse. The Melrose was and is a family run restaurant and so they were happy that we went there as a family as well. I would have my young daughter Alexandra with me and as most parents will know, keeping young children amused when you want to have a nice relaxed but lengthy evening meal is difficult at the best of times. Colouring books soon become coloured in, puzzles soon become too complex or boring, and it's hard for a child to concentrate on reading a book when the adults are becoming increasingly boisterous as the wine takes effect. It was at this stage of the evening that Paul and I would be at our most creative. I think the most inventive of our ideas and one that kept Alexandra amused until it was time for us to exit pretty sharpish (and not go back to the Melrose for some considerable time) involved nylon fishing line and Blue Tack, both purchased from the extremely handy and late opening news and gift shop next door. There were quite a few other diners on the evening in question and with the owners and sole elderly waitress popping in and out of the kitchen at the back of the restaurant, there were numerous occasions when we were left unsupervised. Every time this happened my daughter would make a little more progress on a slow circuit around the room from table to table, and at each stop looping the fishing line round one of the many wall mounted pictures depicting local scenes from a bygone age, fixing the line in place with either Blue Tack or when this ran out a self-made paste of mushy peas, and then draping it across to the next picture ready for tying and sticking when she was next unobserved. After about an hour of this surreptitious adventure we had one end of the line tied to the leg of someone else's table, the rest of the line threaded neatly and invisibly around the entire restaurant encompassing some twenty pictures of varied dimension, two nice vases, some glassware and some ornamental brass frying pans, and the loose end ready for tying to the front door which was to become the 'trigger' when we were ready to leave.

In the end, as we still had loads of wine left to drink, and as we were all too impatient to see what would happen, my brother tied the line to the front door incorporating a coat stand to act as a kind of pulley and we waited expectantly for the next unsuspecting person to either leave the restaurant or enter from the street outside. As an aged couple duly made their exit, I can still remember seeing through a drunken haze and tears of hysterical laughter all twenty pictures swinging maniacally to and fro as if possessed, hearing the vases and glasses smash as they seemingly leapt from their perches of their own free will, and the symbol-like crash of the frying pans as they jumped noisily to the floor. It was like the kitchen scene from Disney's Fantasia where all the utensils come alive and everything goes wrong for Mickey, and somewhere at the back of this hullabaloo were the shrieks of Mrs Melrose, the terrified waitress and the other shocked diners. But looking back on this event, what mystifies me most is the fact there were plenty of other people in the restaurant throughout the evening, so what on Earth they thought my daughter was doing as she made her way stealthily round the room, creeping under their tables and then pretending to take an avid interest in each picture by turn, I will never know. I might just miss those times…

Hobbies and Pastimes

'Ooh look Mavis! There's that man you said was always drunk, what a change has come over him. He does the flower displays for the vicar every week now and I hear they both go trainspotting on the weekend.'

'I like his smart new anorak Doreen, and I'm sure that jumper of his looks like he knitted it himself.'

It might seem strange to include a list of hobbies in a book about having quit alcohol and a bit too anorak for some people, but I do have a reason and I'm not suggesting that having given up booze you need to take up trainspotting, flower arranging in your local church or knitting (not that there is anything wrong with these past-times I hastily add, before the letters of complaint come flying my way).

You are going to have a lot more mental energy and time on your hands once you quit alcohol and it makes sense to use this productively.

What hobbies did I give up?

The short answer is none although I have stopped making my own wine for obvious reasons.

I had been winemaking on and off for years, I started when I was fourteen and was actually encouraged to make it by my mum, bless her. When more recently we lived in the flat I didn't really have the room or the inclination to make any home-made wine, but once we also had the country cottage it was a natural thing to do. Firstly it saved some money, home-made wine works out at about one pound a bottle if made properly (you can make it for about 10% of that but the result is better used as a weed-killer), and secondly it is great fun collecting the fruits and creating something you can enjoy from nature's harvest. You can get an idea of the range of recipes I was concocting from the labels in this picture:

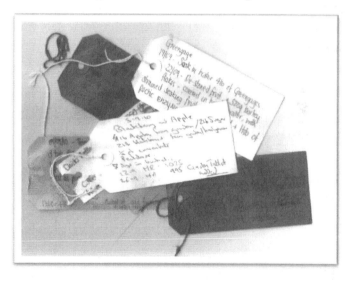

Of course once I quit alcohol there was no longer any point in keeping this hobby going. It made me think what would have happened had I been running a cider making operation or a brewery or something else commercial and drinks based. Would I have had to give that up too? Could I now go and happily get a job in somewhere like that and cope? I think the answer is yes, just like I could run or work in a pub and not be tempted, but I wouldn't want to – I'm simply not interested in anything that involves drink.

So what happened to all the wine I had on the go and which was either in storage or bubbling merrily way in demijohns?

It took me nearly three years after quitting alcohol to get round to throwing it away. I was putting off the day not because I thought I might still need it, but because I was honestly scared smelling the wine might make me want to taste some. Here I am chucking it down the sink:

The kitchen smelt like a wine-farm, and some of the stuff smelt like strong spirits it had been in the demijohn so long. Despite my previous misgivings it was a great feeling pouring it away. I did feel a bit sad about all the equipment I had built up over the years and would no longer use, but I expect it will end up at a car-boot sale one day. I certainly didn't want to taste any of the wine; it certainly didn't make me wish I was still making wine; and if anything, all it did was remind me of the headaches I would sometimes get when I had overindulged, and how the house would sometimes smell in the morning after a particularly heavy party.

What is new, revised or improved?

Astronomy

I have had a telescope for years and part of my university degree was an astronomy course. I even spent a week in Majorca based at the Palma Observatory.

The big problem with astronomy is with it being a nocturnal activity – I was always pissed. Although this didn't stop me taking my telescope into the garden and looking at the stars and planets it did make it precarious. Lugging a heavy telescope around in the dark when you are drunk and at the same time trying to hold a glass of wine without spilling the contents is a recipe for disaster.

Now it's so much easier. I am also happier to stay up later and view the stars in the early hours of the morning. Before, I would only be able to stay up if I also drank. This in turn meant I would still be pissed in the morning leading inevitably to a wrecked day and a hungover feeling late in the afternoon. I never want that experience again. Now of course I can stay up late and still wake up feeling fresh albeit a little tired. It was the Supermoon eclipse this month (September 2015) and my wife and I got up at 2.40 a.m. and went for a long walk to watch the eclipse from a wonderfully dark position on the beach near to where we live (we were still in pyjamas under our coats). We watched the spectacle for an hour and also saw the Milky Way, planet Venus rising and some shooting stars we wished upon. Despite this I was still up and ready for work at 6.30 a.m. and drove to the station as usual feeling thrilled with myself. That would never have happened when I drank.

Writing

Writing is a completely new hobby and something I never imagined I would do, let alone enjoy and possibly even turn into a career.

I started writing stories to fill all the spare time in the evenings I suddenly found I had. Most of these stories were memoirs and involved booze. Whether this was a subconscious cleansing of my mind or not I don't know, but certainly writing those stories gave me a strong 'been there - done that' perspective on my drinking. In fact the feeling was so strong, writing down personal drinking stories has become a major part of my methodology in my book 'I Don't Drink!'

It was my daughter wanting to be an author that stimulated me to explore what was involved in self-publishing a book, and that is what I then set out to do, publishing 'The 7.52 to London Bridge' in 2013.

However, it's only once you have seen your book presented on amazon that the hard work really starts. You have to somehow get people to find your book, you then have to make it stand out enough from the millions of others on offer that they want to have a 'look inside', and you then have to get them to buy it.

For help I joined a local group of authors in my nearest home city who were in a similar position, all having recently self-published, and I still meet with them on a regular basis.

It was the fact we meet in a wine bar, that my book the 7.52 is based so much around drinking tales, and that at the meetings I never drank, that prompted one of the other authors to suggest I write my alcohol related story, and how I gave up drink. It was that suggestion that became 'I Don't Drink!'

Now I write most evenings and love the escape it gives me. At any one time I have at least two books on the go and a myriad thoughts in my head for others still to be written. Even if I never make my fortune from writing, I know my books give pleasure and that my self-help books do just that and help people. Writing also gives me something I can leave to posterity and be forever proud of. It is also nice for my wife to be able to exchange someone who every evening would be drunk and asleep in front of the TV, for a husband who spends his evenings writing books dedicated to **her**.

Question:

What hobbies or pastimes might you take up given lots of extra time, a clear head and guilt-less money to spend on them?

Travel and holidays

I have been fortunate enough to have seen a great deal of the world, both through business travel and an inherent desire to explore. In the latter years of my drinking however, I was finding things increasingly difficult.

Any flight longer than two hours in duration and I would arrive dehydrated and with the onset of gout symptoms. The problem was that despite how much I knew drinking on a plane really dehydrates you badly, I could never bear the thought of flying sober. There is something so natural about getting on a plane, having a gin and tonic, some wine with the food and then perhaps a brandy with the coffee. I have rarely travelled business class but when I have it has also felt natural to have a glass of champagne as soon as you sit down.

What after all is the point of paying so much money if you can't take full advantage of everything on offer?

If I was travelling long haul I would drink at least one of those small bottles of wine every half hour. If this was a ten hour flight to the Far East that meant I was drinking three bottles of wine or thereabouts whilst in the air. I would watch endless films, listen to music and do anything other than sleep so I could enjoy drinking, but I might eventually pass out just before we landed. None of this made any sense if I had to drive at my destination but I never let it stop me.

There are so many business trips I have been on, where I have been at less than my best because of the effects of dehydration and the onset of that gout. There are even more holidays I have ruined because of it.

The worst has to be a romantic trip to Paris with my wife where I had to drag a massively swollen foot around the City. I was in dreadful pain but couldn't complain because we both knew it was self-inflicted. I still feel guilty about letting my drinking ruin that weekend in Paris, it's time I took my wife back there now I am sober and a hundred years younger!

I said I have travelled a lot and I could list countless countries where alcohol and its effects marred the experience. They include a safari in Kenya where I had to use a walking stick, a holiday exploring the national parks across the Western USA where I had to stay on the coach at many of the sites because I couldn't walk, an amazing visit to the pyramids in Egypt where I couldn't even bend down sufficiently or climb the steps to go inside the pyramids themselves, and many a European city break where we had to stay most of the time sitting in the hotel instead of going exploring.

Question:

Are you really happy with every holiday you have been on or has drink had a negative impact as it did for me?

So what is it like flying sober?

Bloody marvellous is the short answer. Have you noticed how much stress you get waiting for the steward/ess to serve the first drink? Waiting whilst they make their way slowly down the aisle. Knowing you are going to have a drink when they finally reach you just makes you more desperate for them to get to you. It is probably like quitting drinking for a month (I wouldn't know), you just can't wait for the month to end so you can get smashed – what a nightmare of stress.

Of course if you are travelling business or upper class you won't be having to wait, but I have been lucky enough to travel business class once or twice and I found it awkward. They give you a glass to drink, you toss it back within seconds and then you either have to wait ages for a top up or you start to feel embarrassed that you have to ask for more, and then more and then more!

Question:

Does waiting for a drink on the plane ever get to you?

Not caring when the trolley gets to you is just one aspect that is so much better without alcohol. The flight itself is more enjoyable, you feel fresher and more relaxed – believe me, it is the opposite of what you imagine where drink would be the thing that relaxes you. And when you get to the other end you are fresh as a daisy, you can far better cope with all the aggravation of customs and getting your baggage, and delays become less of an issue, after all, you are not desperate to get to your hotel for a drink so can take a far more laid-back perspective on events as they unfold. I wouldn't want to go back to travelling drunk ever again.

The really big bonus from flying sober is that with alcohol being a diuretic you dehydrate far less without it, especially as you will be drinking non-alcoholic liquids instead. This was the real killer for me – even if I was flying now and I wanted an alcoholic drink (which I wouldn't), the very thought of all the illness, pain and discomfort the dehydration would cause would be more than enough to make me change my mind.

And the holiday?

We are all different and I suppose it depends what you want from a holiday. In 'I Don't Drink!' I describe some holiday experiences of mine just after I quit drinking. I have never been one (or at least not since I was a teenager) for sitting on a beach getting drunk and listening to someone else's radio blaring away, I have always liked adventure holidays. Having the gout was consequently a nightmare as it stopped me doing things. The only issue I thought I would have was with meal times or being offered complementary drinks when visiting factory shops or wherever on a tour.

I have to say it didn't bother me not drinking. If anything just knowing I was avoiding that awful 'tea-time already feeling a bit sloshed' feeling was enough to convince me I had 'been there and done that' enough times not to want to go there again. But then by that stage I had developed my mind-set to the point where I didn't want a drink anyway, and if you decide to quit forever and you read my book, you will discover exactly what I mean and be able to create a new mind-set for yourself. It works, and to prove the point - a quick aside:

In 2014 I took my family back to South Africa for my youngest daughter's wedding in Cape Town where she was living. Two things essentially drink related stand out about that trip in addition to my coping handsomely at the wedding as a sober father of the bride, something I would have definitely found hard to contemplate had I been answering questions in this book three years ago.

Firstly, that we deliberately visited my wife's and my favourite wine-farm Buitenverwachting in Constantia just so I could stand at the wine-tasting counter, and in front of the somewhat bemused owner of the establishment 'smell' a glass of their wonderful Sauvignon Blanc. If it was an ultimate test I can think of no other and I passed with flying colours, not being the slightest bit tempted to actually swallow any of what before I would have sworn was created by the Gods.

Secondly, we made a huge detour to visit the old mining town of Pilgrim's Rest up north in the region of the Kruger National Park. It was in the town's

Royal Hotel that I was possibly more out of order than I have ever been in my life but somehow and amazingly got away with it.

The event happened in 1970 when I was twenty-three years old, newly divorced and living in Johannesburg. I had met and stupidly got engaged to a girl who was as mad as me and we had decided to go on a road trip to the Kruger. On the way we spent the night at the Royal, and despite its rustic appearance, a very posh hotel at the time in what was seen as one of the leading and most exclusive tourist towns in the region.

The girl and I had been drinking all day despite me driving and it was quite late when we checked into the hotel. In the room we had some champagne whilst we got ready for dinner and we then made our way unsteadily to the candle-lit and very nostalgically decorated restaurant. The only vacant table was in the centre of the room and we duly sat there, ordered some wine, more wine, yet more wine and probably ate nothing other than bread rolls, being too pissed to decide on what proper food to eat. The hotel being full, there must have been at least fifty other smartly dressed guests sat dining that evening.

I imagine you know the feeling when the space around you goes very dark, your vision narrows to the extent you can only see things very close to you and your hearing turns everything more than a couple of feet away into a muffled sound? I think it's called being absolutely blind drunk and well past paralytic. I suppose your brain starts to close down and creates a small window for you to exist through. I got to this stage quite early on in the evening and suddenly desperately needed a pee. You probably know that feeling as well, where you have just seconds to do some drastic or flood your pants. I couldn't even wait to ask the waitress the way to the toilet I was so immediately desperate, and so making my way towards the nearest wall to the left of our table I scrambled my way through some likely curtains and into what I assumed was a corridor where I imagined I found a gent's stand-up toilet, although it seemed a little primitive for such an expensive hotel. I remember peeing and peeing like it would never stop and seeing steam rising from the floor. Another bottle of wine later I had to go again. This time I remember getting stuck in the curtains on the way back and *when I finally freed myself I couldn't even see our table although it was probably no more than five feet in front of me. It is amazing what you do remember of these events.*

The next morning we went into breakfast and as we went to sit at the same table and I looked towards the curtains I quickly realised what I had done the night before. We just upped and fled as fast as we could. The photo below shows me standing at the very same curtains leading to the 'corridor and gent's stand-up toilet I had used!'

How did no one realise what was happening? How did I get away with such appalling behaviour? How come in such a strict country I wasn't put behind bars of even taken out and shot? To use a dreadful pun, it should have been curtains for me! I just had to go back to that spot all those years later just to prove the story to my wife and daughters, and to myself! I should add that behind that curtain is nothing other than the wall, that room is no longer used as a restaurant and thirty years later they have large signs all over the hotel clearly indicating the way to the toilets!

Question:

Have you ever been really 'blind drunk' and what is the worst you have behaved?

It's time for another story...

A story – 'Glass'nost

I have only ever once travelled first class by air, and that wasn't really what you could call first class by modern day or Western standards. It was 1982, I was travelling home to London after some years spent in Africa and I was accompanied by the girlfriend who would subsequently become my second wife for a while. The Soviet airline Aeroflot had by far the cheapest flights available and we had boarded the plane in Zambia in stifling 35 degree heat. The first stop on our journey home was a brief landing at Luanda airport in Angola where we could hear shelling from the civil war currently raging just outside the airport environs. It was from this point on we were bumped up to first class, and once airborne when I peeked through the curtain into the standard class section I could see why.

The rear section was crammed full of so-called Soviet military observers, and a more tough-looking and well-armed bunch of commando type thugs I have only ever since seen in the movies, some even had machine guns and grenade launchers on their laps there being no further room in the overhead racks. After a few hours of flying, the next stop was for fuel at Budapest in Hungary, still at that time a Soviet satellite state, and although we were allowed to leave the plane and stretch our legs we were surrounded by armed soldiers and amazed at the number of Soviet jet fighters stationed at the airfield. And then we landed in Moscow.

In those cold-war days, part of the pleasure of travelling with Aeroflot was a compulsory two night stay in Moscow to appreciate the wonders of communism in action, and to hopefully be converted and want to turn our backs on the capitalist horror that had spawned us. It was mid-winter when we arrived for our indoctrination and -10 degrees which was a massive shock to the system, especially as we were only wearing jeans and t-shirts, not having needed or owned a coat for many years.

Allowing ourselves to be directed by non-English speaking officials and not speaking a single word of Russian ourselves we eventually ended up at a barrack like dormitory of a hotel in central Moscow, and were herded Gulag style into a large room along with fifty or so other weary looking western travellers to hear some anti-everything that wasn't Soviet speeches, and to partake of some what they assumed was 'western style' food which was grim to say the least. Worst of all in this land where we assumed vodka flowed like water there wasn't a bar and there didn't seem to be any way to order drinks with the meal.

Not to be outdone by the red menace, the following morning we left the hotel early. I was on a mission to find a shop that sold booze.

Moscow has a lot to offer with some fascinating history and famous not to be missed monuments which include the Kremlin with its red star topped spires, Lenin's mausoleum in Red Square and St. Basil's cathedral with the candy-stripe minarets. All of this we saw at high speed as we were frozen to the marrow and despite the treacherous icy conditions under foot, ran everywhere. This was not too helpful for the secret agent who attached himself to us as we left the hotel and whose job it was to follow us everywhere, and we lost him within the first five minutes. We also got to travel on the famous metro system because it was nice and warm, and although we had no idea where we were going, the stations themselves with their beautiful stonework and art deco design were a wonderfully refreshing alternative to London's tired looking advertising-poster clad underground system. To say we must have stood out as foreigners and lost souls is probably an understatement, but what really upset me was that despite what we had heard, no-one approached us and offered us a fantastic amount of Rubles for our western clothes and my watch, so having come straight from Africa we really must have looked like shit!

By some miracle we managed to find our way back to our starting point off Red Square and locate the massive GUM department store nearby. With a grand facade somewhat similar to Harrods in London, the equally grand and massive doors of GUM opened onto a chaos of people queuing for whatever was on offer. It looked a bit like the first day of the sales in a bargain basement store back home except that all the women were wearing expensive looking jewellery, dressed in fur coats and high heels and looking far more capitalist than we had ever done, but somehow (probably some sixth sense kicked in) I managed to find the department selling wine and bought what looked to be a bottle of dry white and at what seemed a reasonable price – success.

That evening at dinner time in the camp canteen I summoned over the stern faced akela before she commenced her haranguing of us guests, and asked her if it would be possible for my wine to be opened for me, it not having been possible to make my wishes understood by any other of the staff. All I can assume from her hostile reaction is that having wine with one's meal was not highly thought of in communist Russia, but eventually the deed was done and she eyed me scornfully as I poured myself a glass, gave her my best 'this is how we do things in England' look, and took my first and only sip of the most disgustingly sweet 'dancing-teeth' sherry I have ever tasted in my life. Not daring to reveal my dilemma for fear of being sent to the Siberian salt mines I had to deliberately spill the rest of the bottle on the table.

The next time I met some Russians was also round a drink soaked table but actually in Brighton, at the five star Metropole hotel next to my mother's apartment. I was there with my wife to help a rather portly IT salesman I had met at a conference in Hong Kong, entertain a dozen senior members of the Soviet shipping industry who were visiting the UK to learn about some new computer technology. These Russians really were very high ranking as demonstrated by the fact they were trusted to leave the confines of the Soviet Union in the first place. There were a dozen in all, all men barring one woman who could easily have passed for a man when the lights dimmed. Each represented a different region of this vast communist empire from completely remote and diverse ports such as Murmansk on the Barents Sea within the Arctic Circle, to Odessa on the Black Sea 1500 miles to the south, and Vladivostok opposite Japan some 3500 miles to the east. They also all looked as different from each other as would a table of twelve different African tribesmen. Until later in the evening however, we only ever saw eleven at any one time as one of their member would take his turn to guard the van they had parked outside the hotel behind their coach, and which was full of 'to them' priceless treasures to take back home such as televisions, Western jeans, Scotch whiskey and girlie magazines.

The format for the evening was simply a grand buffet dinner with little else planned as none of the Russians admitted to speaking any English, neither my portly friend or my wife or I spoke a word of Russian, the planned interpreter had failed to materialise and we were relying on our jovial attitude and lots of nodding to make the evening a success. It started well with my friend making sure a large glass of Smirnoff Vodka was placed in front of each guest, and then making a brief speech of welcome which of course they didn't understand but loved, and then we all stood and drained our glasses, slamming them back down on the table in fine Cossack style, we somehow collectively understanding it would have been bad form to smash them against the restaurant wall. Their self-appointed leader, a massive giant of a man from Odessa with an immense black beard covering almost his entire face, then stood and made a similar speech in a deep booming voice, and brought out from somewhere hidden within his copious jacket and passed around a bottle of local vodka from his region for us all to toast with. After three more of these shipping industry magnates had similarly passed around vodka local to their region and made speeches we thought it might be safer to get some food inside us and so the feast commenced.

I have little recollection as to the order of events as the meal progressed but a few things stand out:-

- Wine not being relevant to this particular party, the Metropole wine waiter was sent away to put on ice all the Smirnoff vodka they had in stock.

- Both my wife and I had deep and meaningful conversations with most of the Russians despite the language barrier, and were invited to tour Russia and stay in every port represented – I do so wish we had followed up on this.

- With every speech made more 'special bottles' of vodka appeared from inside coat pockets as if by magic, and glasses were liberally filled by the Russians.

- I made a number of speeches myself, but as my short term memory banks had become restricted to no more than two to three minutes it seems I made the same speech quite a few times.

- At some stage in the evening all the Russians suddenly spoke passable English and admitted to have understood every word we had spoken.

- When the hotel eventually ran dry of vodka we had to move on to Napoleon brandy.

- At one stage, despite the hotel restaurant being full with perhaps twenty or more other busy tables and showing no regard to the protestations of the timid waiters, Blackbeard went over to the sweet buffet, picked up the enormous and heavy cheese board with all its contents and brought it back to our table. He then single-handedly demolished the entire platter.

- There was singing accompanied by swaying in our seats and a waving of knives.

- I somehow managed to get to my feet and make the same speech yet again, and my wife and I attempted to play chopsticks on the nearby grand piano whilst the Russians beat out the tune on the table with their fists.
- One of the Russians who was the spitting image of the French heartthrob singer Sacha Distel made a pass at my wife and then passed out.
- I seem to recall the female Russian punching somebody.

At this stage perhaps because things were getting a little out of hand (and possibly because of the number of complaints) the maitre d' decided we might want to partake of coffee and liquors in the hotel lounge to where we decamped, making ourselves comfortable in a number of sofas positioned around a large glass topped table.

I had been remarkably impressed at how competently my portly friend had managed to stay in control of himself up to this point, perhaps his bulk helped him to cope with the volume of alcohol being consumed, but now it seemed he needed some fresh air. As he stood, walked towards a set of French windows, forced them open and walked outside through the net curtains I remember abstractedly thinking to myself, 'surely they don't lead to the outside balcony, but open instead to a sheer drop to the basement patio two floors below'.

It took perhaps thirty minutes for us all properly to register that our ample host was no longer with us and we decided to instigate a search. With everyone being completely blotto and laughing maniacally like a load of asylum inmates, this included searching beneath chairs, behind lamp stands as if my friend had been three inches wide, and even under cushions as if he had been a set of keys. And then a different set of French windows burst open, our host made a grand entrance but as if in a trance, tottered robotically towards where most of us were still sitting, stood rocking slightly for a second or two and then fell through the glass topped table.

It was a most fitting finale to a wonderful evening and the rapturous applause lasted well past the ambulance people arriving.

Food and Drink

Food

There is no reason why what you eat should be affected just because you don't drink alcohol, but it probably will be.

For one thing there may be particular foods, just like I had with sausages, where drink is so closely associated in your mind you decide you are better either giving them a miss or at least having a break. Similarly there are probably foods you eat as a consequence of your drinking and which you will no longer have a hankering for. A case in point with me is burgers. I very rarely had a burger, but if I was getting a later train home from the City and I needed to sober up I would buy a burger and a milkshake from the Burger King at London Bridge station. At least I didn't consume them on the train in front of other people, something I really hate.

Question:

Do you eat trash food simply to soak up the alcohol?

What you will definitely notice is that your taste buds improve and become more discerning. I have discovered whole new styles of food simply because I now enjoy sampling and exploring the flavours and exploring dishes I would never have bothered to try before. I used to love curry but would always order the same old thing, chicken Madras. Now I try a different style of curry every time we eat out at an Indian Restaurant and on a recent holiday in India I went mad with trying new dishes.

Question:

How adventurous are you with food now? Do you think your enjoyment of food might improve if you quit alcohol or do you worry you might no longer enjoy food without an accompanying drink?

You are also likely to develop a sweet tooth, especially as you will be giving up such a huge sugar intake. It is something you might have to watch, but as alluded to earlier, I lost weight without trying and that despite the additional cakes and puddings I was eating.

Treacle Pudding Syndrome

One thing I did become addicted to when I quit alcohol was treacle pudding. Every single night for perhaps two years I would have to have one. We even collected the little pots they came in to use for Dalek models for our raft in the local Selsey Raft Race.

My over-indulgence in these delicious puddings wasn't really an issue, but when I was making a video with hypnotherapy expert Dan Jones to show my readers via youtube what hypnotherapy was like and how it could help with quitting alcohol, I decided to use my 'addiction' to treacle pud as an example. I didn't use self-hypnosis to help me quit alcohol but 'I Don't Drink!' comes with a superb track from Dan that complements the book and many readers have used it to great effect.

If you watch the video you will see me come up with the idea of using treacle puddings and how I am visibly affected by Dan's words. You can find it on my website.

I have to admit that although I was using the puddings purely for the sake of having something tangible as an example, I have not had a single one since and I don't even have the desire for one! It obviously works.

I also find I get very hungry. Before, perhaps because if I felt even the slightest bit hungry I would have a cider or something else sugary and filling, I never noticed proper hunger pangs. Now I really do.

A further thought on food and drink was brought to mind by a comment made to me by one of my readers. He had been sober for over 100 days and went for a meal at his parent's house where his mum served him home made rum and raisin ice cream. About half an hour afterwards he felt lightheaded and pretty rotten to the extent he didn't feel safe to drive home! He thinks his mother had been overly generous with the rum, and because it was a home environment and despite the name of the dish he hadn't even considered there would be anything alcoholic in it. It is something I look out for, especially as so much food is cooked in wine. I am sure most of the alcohol is leached out in the process but you will probably find that once you decide to quit you too will be anti any alcohol intake at all.

But in summary you **will** enjoy food a whole lot more, especially if you drink water with it, and you might become more selective in what you eat, no longer seeing food as stodge to soak up alcohol but as something to relish and savour. Far more awkward is what to drink.

Drink

I appreciate that for many people and possibly for you as well, deciding what else to drink if you are not going to have something you have been used to for countless years is going to be a serious issue. It has to be something you look forward to having, it has to be as refreshing as that ice cold G&T or that iced beer you usually treat yourself with, and it has to complement the meal you are enjoying with your friends. It's a tall order.

To be honest the best fit I have found, and one that you might also eventually realise as the best fit, is water. If you think about it, for tens of thousands of years until the early tribes in the Middle East apparently farmed animals for milk and then invented beer it's all there was anyway.

I have settled on water and green tea as my main drinks, with a nice fresh coffee with a bun to break up the morning, and lime and soda if I am going out to a bar. The nice thing with the green tea is there are so many varieties to explore and it's good for you, but I appreciate it's not to everyone's taste. Here is a picture from my blog with another suggestion:

15 mile charity walk this afternoon ending up at a nice pub in Chichester. Everyone else was piling in for a pint or some wine and I had a wonderful freshly squeezed lemonade. It was interesting how many of the others changed to have the same as me once they saw and smelled how refreshing it was.

When I first quit alcohol I did tarry with non-alcoholic beers and wines. I avoided the low alcohol ones simply because they are what they say they are and they do contain alcohol.

The beers I swiftly found gaseous and boring and the wines were nothing special so I stopped having any of these substitute style drinks and they are not inexpensive either. I also think they are aimed more towards the drinker who can't drink that day for whatever reason rather than someone who doesn't drink at all, after all what is the point of pretending to drink when there are zillions of other non-alcoholic drinks to try. Mind you, if you are really worried about how you are going to cope at that wedding or party you have to go to, or you simply can't face the idea of having a curry without a beer to accompany it, the fact there are non-alcoholic wines and beers available and that the quality of these continues to improve, is a real help.

Question:

Have you tried non-alcoholic beer and wine?

How did you cope with this as a substitute or do you think you will quickly become bored with it?

Some more drink suggestions

My friends at **Club Soda** have kindly put together their own list of drinks you might want to try together with some comments against each of these. You can find this list at the end of the book in the chapter: Club Soda – some non-alcoholic drink suggestions.

I also tell you a little more about this great group of people who are well worth following and meeting up with.

Friends and family

In my view, by far the most important aspect of one's life is the relationship you have with those you love. There are some difficult questions to answer in this chapter, and some awkward things to consider, I make no apologies for that.

From a day to day perspective I like to think I have been a nice person to be around, although I do discuss this some more in the chapter towards the end of this book which looks at whether or not I would have been able to live with someone like me. And of course everyone is fundamentally different regardless of whether they drink or not. I am therefore going to focus on one aspect of change only, and something that will be impacted no matter what your personality is like, **time**.

Time spent now

If my wife or children wanted me to sit down and have a 'serious' conversation with them I would open a bottle of wine first, 'to help me concentrate!'

It's when you see people smoking around their children that you tend to notice time being mis-spent. I remember when I used to smoke and my children were infants, I would hear myself say so often 'in a minute' or 'let me just finish my cigarette'. Now when I witness children needing attention and I hear others say that, I really do want to scream at them 'put the bloody cigarette out!' I know I was like that and I know I was like that with drink, I would either want to finish my glass of wine first, or I would be too busy looking for the waiter at a restaurant or I would be too busy 'whatever' to focus my attention on where it should have been directed, at the people with me.

Now I have far more time for others and it's not just because I'm not too busy drinking to give them my attention, it's as if a whole world of pressure and urgency has been lifted from my shoulders. There is no nagging 'get this done and then you can have a drink' being whispered into my subconscious by some drink devil, and he isn't saying 'you need a drink to relax and escape' either. The drink devil has gone and he is not coming back! I even remember if my wife or children wanted me to sit down and have a 'serious' conversation with them I would open a bottle of wine first 'to help me concentrate'. What utter crap! I can now see this was just that damned drink devil telling me alcohol was the best way of dealing with stress whereas the reality is it's the last thing you need to relieve stress!

Without that devil I know I am far more laid back than I ever was. I have more patience with people, I am more aware of things and I therefore tend to spot issues that others might have, so I can step in and try to help. It must be that by not being mentally addicted to anything I can cope far better with whatever comes my way. There are no longer any barriers.

But this doesn't mean I have become a pushover, I am far less likely to suffer fools or rudeness or hurtful behaviour from others because I am now far more likely to say something. The big difference is now it is me talking and not drink talking, I can be far more rational in what I say and how I get my views across, and I get listened to and taken far more seriously.

I have also become far less selfish in my attitude to others, and that goes much broader than close friends and family. I can actually hear myself being nicer to people and expressing an interest in people I might have ignored before, purely because I always seemed to have something pressing on my mind. That damned devil again or was it the fact I was too pissed to concentrate on anything but myself and my own immediate selfish needs.

The other thing that drinking does of course (unless you only drink at home) is probably take you away from your loved ones to a pub or wine bar or wherever it is you feel you need to go to escape – and what is it people are escaping from? I think when I used to spend night after night in a wine bar I was only ever escaping from myself.

Question:

Do you ever hear the drink devil whispering to you and creating an urgency that doesn't really exist?

Does the drink devil encourage you to drink to cope better with stress?

> **If you think drink helps you deal with stress - think again!**
>
> **It might be what people tell you and what you read but don't believe it for a second, it simply is <u>not</u> true**

Do you feel that you give less time to your loved ones as a result of drink?

Have you heard yourself dismiss other people's needs or have ignored a child's request for attention because you are too busy drinking and too busy to care?

A Hard Challenge:

How about sitting your family down in a nice relaxed setting and asking them what they honestly think about your drinking? I bet you won't dare do it, because you already know what the answer will be, and you probably know they will hide some of the truth anyway. And it might just force you to HAVE to do something about your drinking.

Time for later

These were the last words I remember my brother speaking to me. He had been taken into hospital for the first time and I had been sent an urgent text from his girlfriend to call him. I recall telling him I couldn't see him that day as I was doing the annual charity 5,000 metre swimathon, something he had managed to do with me a few years before, and had been very proud of achieving.

'I wish I was doing that too' he said, and I could hear the sorrow in his voice.

He was dead within a few short weeks. He had let himself out from hospital, gone back to being a wreck and then been taken back into the hospital to die. He was in a coma the next time I saw him and he died that night.

He didn't just miss out on the swimathon, he missed out on a whole lot more besides:-

- He missed out on seeing his daughters again, who had years before been taken to live in America but who are now reunited with us thanks in part to the power of the internet.
- He missed out on knowing about, let alone

seeing, watching grow up, and spending precious moments with the wonderful grandchildren he now has.

- He missed sharing my two daughter's weddings with me.
- He missed out on being a great-uncle to my grandson.
- He missed knowing there **is** a life after alcohol and that it is a million times better than the one he was living.
- He missed out on who knows how many years of life, adventures, celebrations, surprises, experiences and happiness.

And he missed out on **all** his life's wishes. They all died with him that day in the hospital bed.

But we all also miss out on him! There are so many times I say 'Paul would have loved this', or 'Paul would have known how to do this' and 'what a shame Paul is not here to see this', and more besides - but he isn't here. It's the same with my mum – she missed out on my daughter's weddings, her great grandchildren, seeing me change my life and become an author, sharing wonderful times with us all, and we all miss her being with us. She was from a family where all the women lived until a great age and she was the same age as the Queen, so there is no reason why she shouldn't still be here enjoying everything we do with us. If only she hadn't succumbed to drink. Sometimes any sorrow I have for my Mum and my brother is heavily tainted with anger!

Question:

What do you wish for and hope to enjoy in your future years?

How sad would you feel if you knew drink had got the better of you, you were dying, and that so many of your life's wishes were going to be unfulfilled or that you were leaving everyone you loved behind in a world that was incomplete?

Do you ever talk about the distant future with your family and plan things together, and have you considered that they might already worry you won't be around to share the reality of your plans with them?

What would you say to your family about their future if you were dying because of your drinking?

> I would swap everything for an extra day of LIFE with my wife and family

Philosophy

I think about things much more often than I ever did before, and far more deeply. It's not just having time to think, it's a great deal more than that. I mention much earlier in the book that the new life you feel when you quit alcohol is like being told you no longer have cancer or a similar life threatening disease, and perhaps that is what provides that new spark, and that new desire to live every second of your life to the full.

It doesn't mean you have to go berserk and fill every second with a 'bucket list' style activity, but for me it has heightened my desire for learning, for discovering new things about mankind and the world we inhabit, about me, and about what happens after I die.

I have always paid lip service to being just that little bit religious and steered my leanings towards the Buddhist doctrine but I don't go to any church or temple, I don't belong to any sect or gathering and I don't worship. But I do pray and I do wish for things. Incidentally the picture above, I took at Bagan in Burma and on the far horizon is the magically named river Irrawaddy. If ever a sight justified mankind ever having existed on this planet it is the sheer scale of the place and the vision of the ancient builders of Bagan, and yet the complete harmonious serenity of it all and it's sympathetic embrace with nature.

I studied a lot of fascinating science for my degree, especially the cosmology and quantum aspects and they instilled in me three things of consequence:-

1. That there has to be sophisticated life on other planets somewhere in this impossibly vast universe.
2. That for the quantum effects we are able to measure to be explainable, there have to be further dimensions than the four we perceive at our macro level of the World.
3. That the existence of an infinite number of parallel universes explains many of the phenomena I myself have experienced.

If all that sounds a bit deep don't worry, I am not going to try and sell anything to you. It merely serves to emphasise the new philosophy I have to life since having quit alcohol and given myself this new and unexpected opportunity. But there are two aspects of that philosophy that may be worth sharing.

*One, that there **has** to be something driving everything or is there really no point at all to the Universe? And that if there is a bigger picture, although we are unable to comprehend what that is, even those of us who call it God, it's safe to say that the more we learn about ourselves and the happier we are in ourselves the better placed we are to play a more integrated part in that bigger picture.*

Secondly, making time for ourselves is crucial despite being seemingly impossible for those of us living within a fast paced western culture. Perhaps one advantage of having been a drinker is that now I no longer am, I really appreciate the difference in the amount of time I have available for myself and for others, and how much more I understand that time is infinitely more important than any amount of money or possessions.

If this is the one positive thing I CAN take away from having been an alcoholic, it was worth it.

There is so much that is outstandingly amazing about every aspect of everything and everyone around us, even at the sub-atomic level, it would be a crime to waste a single second of my life thinking anything other than positive thoughts, regardless of the provocation otherwise, and it would be a crime to limit my time in this existence due to wanton misuse of the shell carrying my spirit. I will learn what I can whilst I am here, so I can pass on with no regrets and hopefully leave something lasting of myself for others to benefit from. It's one of the reasons I currently write.

I don't want to end up like my brother, lying on my death-bed and wishing I was doing things I can't purely because of my own stupidity and selfishness.

Question:

How much time do you spend contemplating the bigger picture?

What legacy do you want to leave behind?

Conclusions

We have covered a lot of ground in the above section and encouraged you to ask a lot of questions of yourself. You doubtless have far more issues and aspects you would want to explore and that I have not identified simply because we are all individual. But I hope this has provided a good enough platform for you to work from.

We have discussed the work environment. We've thought about what opportunities you might have lost, and what relationships you might have soured because of drink. But we've also considered your aspirations career wise and how achievable these will be, both if you stay as you are and if you quit alcohol.

We looked at how much drinking currently costs you and considered what or on whom this money can be far better spent.

We considered the health impact of alcohol and how your lifespan might be seriously affected if you don't quit alcohol, what this means to others, and how that same lifespan can be hugely extended by quitting alcohol.

We talked about fitness, hobbies and past-times, and entertainment and how these will be massively improved and enhanced with you no longer being drinker.

We looked at travel and holidays and considered the positives from not being a drinker despite some of the misgivings you might have.

We discussed food and drink and how your taste buds will improve, and looked at some ideas for what you can drink as a replacement for your usual tipple.

Most importantly we identified some areas where your relationship with those you love will be enhanced through you having more time, patience and understanding, once the drink devil leaves you in peace. And I hopefully encouraged you to think about what you and others will sadly miss out on if you shorten your life through something which is firmly in your power to resolve.

And finally I asked you to consider what you might want to think or philosophise about given so much more time for **yourself** as well.

> **I swapped a 5 year life expectancy for a 45 year life expectancy – with very few limits on what I can do!**

But I also included some stories to prove I have 'been there and done that', and rest assured as my friends will vouch for, just because there is no longer alcohol involved it doesn't mean I have any less maniac or enjoyable a time – the big difference now, is that I always remember what happened and what I did, and barring injury there are no painful consequences!

> **Just because there's no longer alcohol involved it doesn't mean I have any less maniac or enjoyable a time – but the big difference now, is I remember what happened!**

Now, to conclude the book I want you to look at yourself from someone else's perspective. Then, hoping you do decide to quit, I tell you what my first day of being a non-drinker was like, and we look at some of the options going forward.

Could you live with YOU?
How would you like it?

This is necessarily an incomplete chapter. I wanted to write my wife's perspective on me being a drinker and put across her point of view. When I approached her on this however she refused. She said 'there are things best forgotten, there are things that hurt so much at the time you really don't want me to go there again and confront you with them now. Just leave it at that!'

Naturally this scared me. I knew I had never been violent when drunk, I don't think I have ever hit anyone in my life. I knew I had been silly and probably said things I shouldn't have done, but I had obviously behaved in a way that caused pain and embarrassment and for that I am truly sorry. I can't even blame the drink because the drinking was my fault.

I know sometimes my wife would tell me not to be nasty and I think I was perhaps nasty, but usually because I either thought I needed (wanted) a drink, or when I later had had too much to drink, I perhaps felt guilty and so blamed the world and everyone in it. Maybe I was too drunk to care, and how terrible is that.

So would I like to live with someone like my old self?

And I base this section purely on what I **know** I was like – there must have been a lot more to my behaviour and attitude besides, and that people don't want to tell me about.

- Would I cope living with someone who got nasty for no apparent reason? Or when I said they had had too much to drink snapped my head off?

- Would I enjoy being sober and sitting watching TV with someone drunk and falling asleep snoring?

- Would I like to go to a party or a public event and be with someone who was obviously drunk and being rude because they thought it was funny? Would I not feel intensely embarrassed and ashamed by this?

- Would I like to spend my day anxiously hoping the person I lived with wasn't going to get drunk that day and ruin everything?

- Would I be happy going short of money because my partner was spending thousands of pounds every year on booze?

- Would I put up with someone who couldn't remember what they had done or said the day before because they were drunk?

- Would I put up with the broken promises, the phoning to say they will be late home as something has come up, when I know it is because they are out drinking.

- Would I put up with someone blaming their drinking on stress, work pressures, or the premise that alcoholism is a disease when it isn't, it's purely because they can't face reality and fix for themselves something that is eminently fixable?
- Would I put up with knowing someone is steadily drinking themselves to an early grave and not caring enough about me to do anything about it?

The answer to all the above has to be a very emphatic NO!

I am so lucky to be so loved, because I wouldn't have put up with me!

I used to work in a pub in my early twenties, a really nice old fashioned English pub in a beautiful little village. I hated all the men who came in and just sat at the bar on their own, looking for someone to moan to. They would complain about their wives or their children and say no one understood them. I used to think 'why don't you go home for once instead of sitting here every night you damned fool.' The same people would come in every night. To a great extent it is why I have never really frequented pubs much ever since, especially not on my own (wine bars were different in my view, but probably only because there wasn't a counter to sit at), I always hated to see the losers sat at the bar ready to complain about their life. **Was I really one of those losers once?**

Question:

What do you think you are like to live with? Go on, really analyse yourself and try completing my check list. Hopefully you won't get too low a score. Then imagine living with a double of yourself, and having to cope with your double from the perspective of a sober observer / partner?

Negative trait	Comment	Opposite positive trait	1 = nasty / 10 = nice
Nasty		Nice natured	
Short with people	Tetchy and tense	Accommodating	
Impatient		Patient	
Aggressive		Placid	
Violent		Calm	
Self-centred	Not thinking of others	Thoughtful of others	
Too busy	Especially where giving children are concerned	Makes time for others	
Forgetful		Organised	
Slapdash	Especially where DIY is concerned	Methodical	
Boring	unadventurous	Exciting	

I put this list together based on some of the traits my wife said I had when I was drinking. I have also been through the list with my wife and eldest daughter from the position of what I'm like now versus what I used to be like. I am delighted to say my score has risen markedly. The traits that have changed most significantly for the better are impatience, forgetfulness, my being short with people, being too self-centred and being too busy to give enough time to others. I recognise that most of these negative traits were driven by my focus on where my next drink was coming from and when.

It is interesting that had I been asked to complete this list when I was half-cut, I know I would have scored myself very highly on every positive trait. It just goes to show how often we see ourselves in a different light from the way others see us when we are drunk.

Challenge:

Assuming you tried thinking through this list sober, try it again when you have had a few drinks!

My first day

That first day I gave up alcohol was Hell!

That first day I gave up alcohol was hell. Not because the giving up drink was hell but because I felt like hell. I had a hangover which meant a splitting headache and I had gout which meant acute pain every time I tried to move my left foot or my knees.

My eldest daughter and son-in-law had been staying with us and were still there that morning so I had to make the effort to get out of bed and go downstairs, and once there I just sat with a glass of water feeling awful and ashamed at the condition I was in.

The only saving grace I had was in my head. I kept saying over and over to myself – 'Never again. This is the last day I will ever feel like this because I will never ever drink again.' I had said these things to myself before of course, probably hundreds if not thousands of times over the years, but this time it was different – the message was for me and for me alone. I didn't and wouldn't say anything to anyone else, I wouldn't do the usual 'I am quitting drinking!' announcement purely to receive the derision that message so rightly deserved, no, this time I would keep the knowledge secret to me and tell no-one until they noticed I hadn't been drinking. Then I would drop into conversation the fact I had quit.

I sat quiet for most of that day, planning how I would quit, and going through all the things that would make up my methodology and that are set out in my book 'I Don't Drink!' I started making lists of things I would need and things I would need to remember, but most of all, I determined the one big thing I was going to focus on – gout. I was going to beat gout and change my life. I was not going to die before my time like my brother had, I would beat gout and by so doing, live and be healthy.

I sat quieter still and thought some more. My wife remembers me cowering into myself as if I was a crab withdrawing into my shell, and it probably looked that way.

A far better analogue to look back on is me being a caterpillar creating a chrysalis, because just as happens in the insect world once I emerged from that cocoon there was no way back. I would be something and someone new!

As I sat there planning I wanted to shut the day and everyone in it out, and I so wished that day could be over so I could start the first real day of my life. I was even counting down the hours until bed-time.

I drank gallons of water that day, I tried to flush every drop of alcohol I had ever drunk from my system. I imagined my poor liver getting just that little bit better because of the water and my drinking nothing alcoholic. I told it I would try harder and drink lots of water every day from there on.

To be honest I thought about drink a lot that day, not from the perspective of wanting a drink but what I would miss. I thought about the nice times that involved drink such as a glass of cider after a hard swim, or a refreshing glass of wine sitting by the beach. I had to keep reminding myself I had been there and done that and focus back on the negatives such as the gout and not wanting to die.

By tea-time I felt a little better although my knees were still swollen and I carried on with the water diet. My wife looked at me quizzically and must have wondered when I was going to have some wine, but mercifully she didn't say anything, because I didn't want to explain what I was doing.

The strangest thing is it felt like I was being watched that day. It felt as if someone or something was focusing on me and testing my resolve. Perhaps it was my subconscious working overtime and talking to my conscious self – telling me there was no way back, and that this thing had to be done!

I went to bed very early that night. I remember laying back with my head on the pillow and smiling to myself. By this time I had given up thinking about wanting a drink or the drinks I would miss because there was no point, there was no countdown that had started until the time I could drink again, this was it, forever. As I lay there staring at the ceiling there was already a strange and unexpected calm coming over me. In retrospect I believe it was the lack of mental planning about booze that was so refreshing. I wasn't doing any of my normal 'didn't drink today so I can have extra tomorrow' routine. All that had been switched off by my subconscious as being irrelevant.

This really was day one of a whole new life. Nothing would ever be the same again, and I couldn't wait for the next day to begin. I had found a calendar I would use as a non-drinking star chart to reward myself with a star each day and I had even found a packet of stars to stick on! The first thing I was going to do when I woke up was stick on that first star and count one!

I knew it might be a difficult journey I was taking, I knew there would be trials and tribulations and even regrets perhaps, but I was determined. This new 'forever' was an unknown alien world I would face in the morning, but I was ready to meet it head on. If someone then had told me how easy a journey it would turn out to be, I would have laughed in their face.

> Nothing would ever be the same again, and I couldn't wait for the next day to begin!

Thinking of joining me?

The object of this book has been to make you think about how drink is affecting your life and to help you appreciate what a fantastic difference life is without the burden of alcohol. I haven't challenged whether or not you are an alcoholic or just someone who drinks too much, and I haven't harped on about the health dangers from drinking alcohol, but I hope I have helped you to envisage a new you that could emerge if you decide to create your own chrysalis and then break out into a fresh and exciting world.

So if some of this book has made you seriously think about quitting alcohol, there are some options to consider:

Cutting down your intake.

I thought about this the other day whilst out walking with my wife and she happened to mention she would like a glass of champagne. My wife hardly ever drinks and perhaps has two to three glasses of champagne a year at most, she only ever really drank just to keep me company when I was at my most wreck-head stage many years ago.

It wouldn't bother me her having some drinks because I know she wouldn't get drunk and boring like I used to be and anyway why shouldn't she get her own back? But she was only saying she wanted some champagne as an idea, she didn't really want an actual drink at all.

I said to her that one day I might get to the stage where I can have the occasional glass of champagne and not be tempted to have more. But then I thought about what I had said. I could taste the champagne as I pictured the glass in my hand and I knew if ever I had the one glass, I would have to have a whole bottle. I told my wife this and jokingly said we could perhaps have a bottle once a week, maybe on Saturdays as a special treat. But I knew I would quickly convince her Friday was a better day for a treat and so we would have a bottle on the Friday, but then I would convince her the Saturday was more relevant after all, so we could have another bottle on the Saturday. We laughed how I would also suggest we round off the weekend with a special bottle of champagne on the Sunday. Then I knew it would shortly lead to having a bottle every day. Then I knew I would soon be having two to three bottles per day, and within a few short weeks I would be back where I started – a complete alcoholic wreck.

> **If you really feel you can cut down your intake and stick to a new regime, you are a better person than I!**

Quitting for a fixed period

Many people I know try the 'Dry January' or 'Sober October' approach to managing their alcohol intake. The unlucky ones come across people like me half way through their month off. I would be the pain that kept saying things like 'It's not as if you are giving up forever, so getting pissed tonight won't hurt you. You can always do an extra day at the end of the month.' Just the kind of friend you don't need.

I sort of gave up drinking for fixed periods when I gave up smoking over twenty years ago. The only way I could quit smoking was to not drink during the week and I only allowed myself to drink on Saturday and Sunday. It worked for a while and I certainly gave up smoking cold turkey, but by Saturday lunchtime I would be smashed. As part of my no smoking regime I kept a daily star chart to log my success and I also used the chart to note with an 's' how often I went for a swim, it was the swimming that played a major part in helping me to quit. I recently found the old chart I had used, to scan a copy to put in 'I Don't Drink!' and it was confusing to note that every Saturday my wife had put a 'p'. Neither of us could remember what the p was supposed to represent until she recalled it stood for 'paralytic'. It just shows to what extent I was binge drinking on the Saturday to make up for all those sober weekdays. In any event it seems I was soon back to drinking every day but at least I have never smoked since.

When I think back I can remember how I felt all those years ago. I recall feeling fit and healthy by about Wednesday and enjoying not drinking, but that I would be dreaming of the weekend and having all that lovely wine and cider. Sometimes I would even hold a bottle in my hand and relish the thought of drinking it in two day's time. Sometimes I would be in a meeting or listening to a conversation but my thoughts would be elsewhere. 'Just 48 hours to go' I would think to myself, 'Just another 48 hours and I can have a well-deserved drink.' It's this attitude that convinced me I could never give up for a month or any other fixed period.

> **I would always be dreaming of the day**
>
> **I could drink again**

I have discussed this with the friends of mine who undertake 'Dry January', and with readers who have written to me on the subject and it seems almost everyone is the same. They can't imagine giving up forever, because they know how much they long for the day they can a drink again when they do their fixed period sabbatical. If you read some of the blogs that are there to support dry month regimes you will see many of the posts carry a similar theme, 'only a week to go and then I am planning to get hammered with my mates!'

Question:

Have you tried a dry month and did you focus on when you would be able to drink again?

Did you picture in your mind a nice big glass of cold white wine, a long refreshing beer, or the wonderful look and aroma from a gin and tonic with ice and a slice?

I do wholeheartedly support the dry month regimes for those that can stick to it but it was never for me. They are great for people who want to lose a little weight or give their body a rest from all the toxins, but it isn't really solving the bigger issue is it.

Dry forever

For me, for a great many other people I have spoken to, and for readers of 'I Don't Drink!' who have taken the time to write to me, this is by far the easiest approach. I know that cutting down or doing a dry month by comparison would be sheer torture – forever thinking about and building a mental picture of that next drink and counting down the days and hours. When you decide to go dry forever there simply is no point in thinking about drink at all. That simple knowledge directs all your future mental thought processes.

- There is no point thinking about drink so you don't.

- There is no point being envious of others when you see them drinking or when you hear about their drinking exploits because you have 'been there and done that', and now you don't.

- There is no point in looking back wistfully and wishing 'if only' because this is it – a new life. What's done is done.

- There is literally everything and every aspect of your life to look forward to in a hugely positive and fresh new light.

- There are the wonderful new relationships to look forward to once those you love know you will be dry forever.

- There are all those myriad benefits from not drinking to discover, and all with the sure guarantee that none will be subsequently undone because this is only a temporary measure.

- There is the knowledge that **you have given yourself** the chance for a new life, far more years in which to live it, and that you have achieved something so many people regard as virtually impossible and will be amazed by.

- There is the absolute pleasure of being able to proudly say 'I don't drink!'

- There is the fact that every single day gets better, easier, more enjoyable and more fulfilling.

> 'Wow that's incredible. You have been three years
> without a drink! I would love to be able to say that!'

Still not sure?

A final task

*If you didn't do so as you read through the book, list
what you think or now know the benefits to you and
issues you may have from quitting drinking will be.
Go over the chapters and the questions in this book
again if that helps and highlight those that relate to
you.*

*Now list any downsides you can think of from giving
up, and feel free to add the fact you don't or didn't
really want to give up.*

Which list is the longest and strongest?

What is this list clearly telling you?

And a final and truthful reminder:

> No matter how hard you find it to contemplate right now – you really <u>won't</u> miss drinking once you quit forever!

To end with an analogue related to the title of this book, whichever road you decide to take, I wish you good luck on your journey. If you decide to quit alcohol forever I know you will be able to do it and have the will to succeed, because even I did it, and I know you will one day soon look back and relish the day you decided to revolutionise your life and change <u>everything</u> for the better. You have already made a start by reading this book, so even if it takes some time for you to take the next step, well done and please keep in touch.

And as my late brother used to say:

God Bless

'I Don't Drink!'

If you have enjoyed this book, found it useful and have decided to quit alcohol forever, then my book 'I Don't Drink!' will help.

I contains my methodology, lots of discussion and advice, more amusing stories and a day-to-day guide to help you through the initial stages.

You can find out more, purchase the book and follow my blog at:

www.idontdrink.net

Club Soda – some non-alcoholic drink suggestions

An important consideration in giving up alcohol is what you are going to drink instead. Laura Willoughby, the founder of Club Soda has kindly put together a list of non-alcoholic drink suggestions based on her and some of the Club Soda member's favourites:-

There are all sorts of awesome soft drinks and exciting mocktails you can get hold of, but generally when you actually get to a pub, the options are somewhat less than thrilling. The good news is that things are improving with the growth of non-drinkers and the necessity of having something for the designated driver.

Here are some things that you might actually be able to get hold of at your local:-

Kopparberg – Kopparberg make a non-alcoholic pear cider that is available from some Wetherspoons. The good news is that it tastes pretty much the same as regular Kopparberg. The bad news is that Kopparberg is one of those ciders that's about 80% sugar. So whether you will appreciate this offering is pretty much determined by whether or not you like normal Kopparberg.

Beck's Blue – this seems to be the most widely available of the non-alcoholic beers. It is mentioned in our non-alcoholic beer tastings www.joinclubsoda.co.uk/no-alcohol-beers but it's not exactly covered in glory. There are a few bars that also do Erdinger Alkoholfrei, and we have seen the odd bottle of Rothaus Tannenzapple Alkoholfrei in real ale pubs. It's always worth asking to see what they have.

Lime and Soda – this seems to be the go-to for every non-drinker out there. Probably because you can get it anywhere and it's not particularly sweet. We are collecting details of the price your local charges as part of our #limeandsoda watch, do let us know on Twitter what you have been charged

Lime and Cranberry – a variation on the above.

Water – you will be very well hydrated and a cheap date!

Fruit Juices – most bars will stock at least a few fruit juices. Here is an opportunity to get yourself a Virgin Bloody Mary, or at the very least an orange juice and soda. Fun fact: Apparently this is called a 'King Henry'. You could also order a grapefruit juice and soda for something less sweet. Or an orange juice and bitter lemon, sometimes called a St. Clements.

Tonic Water – you can call this a T&T if you want to be cute and you don't think your friends will hurt you. You can also add lots of non-alcoholic things to it, especially if the bar is specialising in cocktails. Ask what bitters they have, a few (and we mean a few) drops of angostura bitters should be easy, but fingers crossed for a more exotic cherry or chocolate. Grenadine and other 'cordial' type coffee cocktail ingredients also work well. You should also check our website for our tonic recommendations.

Ginger Beer – of the easily available soft drinks for the non-drinker, ginger beer is possibly the best. You might even luck out and find a place that stocks one of our top picks. Just make sure they don't give you one of those tiny bottles of Schweppes ginger ale (not the same thing!) or one of the new alcoholic ones.

Lemonade – or bitter lemon ideally. Or bitter lemon and sprite (or soda water) if you feel like a lemony compromise (or a quinine boost).

j20 – j20 is awful. I don't know who it's for. It sort of looks like it should be for adults but it has the sugar content of Brazil.

Appletiser – it's basically the same as an apple juice and soda. I happen to like that.

<u>**Now have a look around your local bar**</u>.

Do they do cocktails? If they do, you are in luck because there is more or less bound to be at least one softail option.

Do they have bitters? Bitters is a non-drinker's best friend. It kills the over-sweetness which is the bane of soft drinks. We already suggested putting it in your tonic, but really you can add it to almost anything. Mixed with ginger beer and lime and ice it makes a Gunner, which is a satisfying alternative to drinking.

Is there tea or coffee? Better yet is there Irish Coffee? Because where there is Irish Coffee there is coffee you can drink through a thick layer of cream. Which is frankly a delight.

Rebel – you can also experiment with bringing your own cordials to the pub and simply adding them to soda. So keep your eyes peeled for our awesome cordial suggestions.

Club Soda

Club Soda are a great bunch of fun-loving people I have joined to help others face up to and beat alcoholism. The approach Club Soda take is fresh, new, non-moralising and definitely anything but preachy.

Club Soda Mission

Club Soda exists to help people to be happier and healthier by changing their drinking; whether they want to cut down, stop for a bit, quit or stick.

Club Soda Vision

We want to be the trusted place to go to for information, tools and support to help people take a self-guided journey to changing their drinking. We will connect people who want to change their drinking with others who can support them in doing that, both fellow members and experts.

For more information or to join Club Soda go to:

www.joinclubsoda.co.uk

Copyright

Also by the author

THE 7:52 TO

LONDON BRIDGE

A COMMUTER'S TALES OF
ADVENTURE AND MISADVENTURE

JULIAN KIRKMAN-PAGE

Now available from amazon

and

www.the752tolondonbridge.com

14460188R00137

Printed in Poland
by Amazon Fulfillment
Poland Sp. z o.o., Wrocław